Weaving

In easy steps

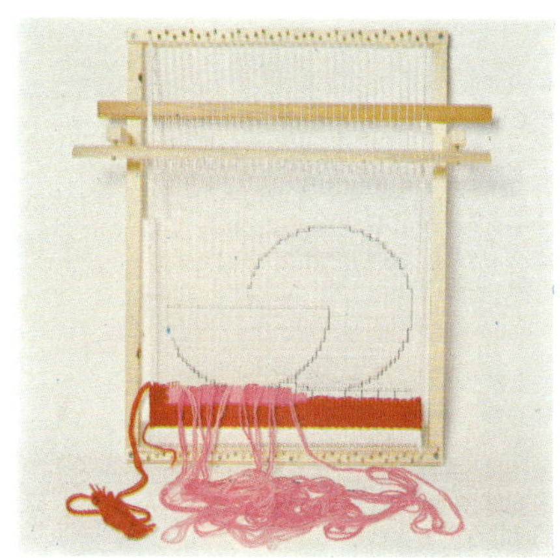

Weaving
In easy steps

Hilary Chetwynd

 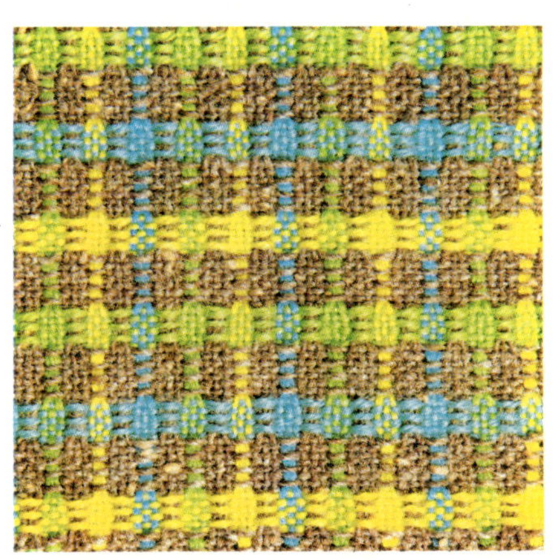 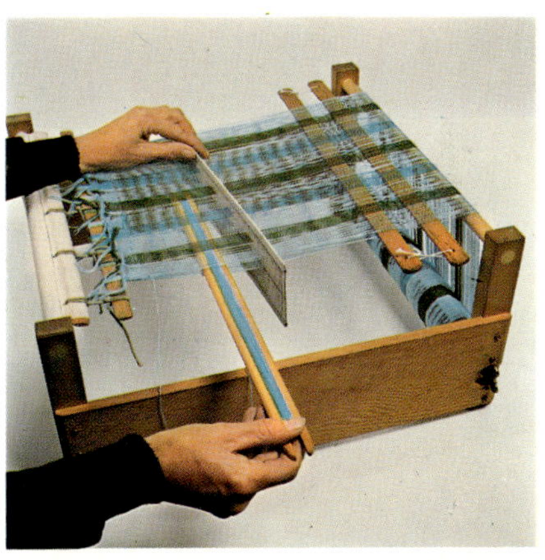

Studio Vista
London

Written by Hilary Chetwynd
Photographs by Peter Kibbles

A Studio Vista book published by
Cassell & Collier Macmillan Publishers Ltd.,
35 Red Lion Square, London WC1R 4SG
and at Sydney, Auckland, Toronto, Johannesburg,
an affiliate of
Macmillan Publishing Co. Inc.
New York.

ISBN 0 289 70759 5

Set in Times Roman by Amos Typesetters, Spa Road, Hockley, Essex, England.

Printed by Sackville Press Billericay Limited, Billericay, Essex, England

Contents

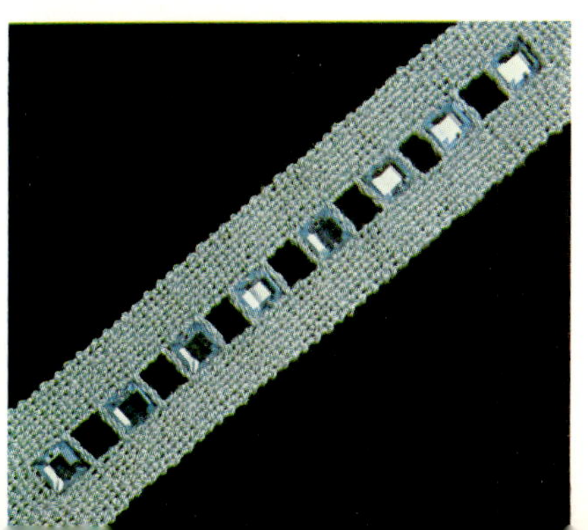

Introduction to Weaving

Some of the tools and materials you can use for weaving. Many of these can be made at home with the most elementary knowledge of carpentry. All the yarns used in the following projects were dyed at home in a small kitchen on a normal stove.

Top, from left to right: Raffia. Rug frame with white cotton warp, leashes and lease stick in position. Tapestry frame with rod for leashes resting on dresser hooks. Hank or skein winder. Spools of coloured cotton. Inkle loom. Spindle.

Centre, from left to right: Ball winder. Wooden box with nails set at each end for box weaving, containing balls of home-dyed wool. Stick shuttle. Picture frame and coloured straws for picture weaving. Roller shuttle. Yarn spool holder. Hank and balls of pink and red home-dyed wool. Rigid heddle loom. Rigid heddle and raw fleeces in centre of loom. Balls of green and yellow yarn. Hank of dip-dyed sisal string.

Front, from left to right: Tape measure. Reed hook. Two threading hooks. Pair of scissors. Set of cards for card or tablet weaving. Rigid wooden heddle.

To start weaving your equipment need not be complicated. A wooden box, an old picture frame, a piece of board, some pins and nails and a little imagination is sufficient. When you have experimented and found that you enjoy weaving, this could be the time to buy a loom. The size you choose will depend on the type of fabric you wish to make and the amount of space you have. It is no more difficult to weave on a large loom or frame than a small one.

You can weave with a great variety of threads, for example, raffia, sisal and other strings, coloured wires and electric cables, grass, straw, strips of paper, or homespun yarn. Dyeing your own yarn with chemical dyes is a simple process if you combine the instructions given here with those on the dye container.

Weaving is the interlacing of threads to form a structure. Woven fabric consists of warp and weft threads interlaced. The warp threads lie parallel along the length of the fabric and the weft threads lie across the width of the warp threads. There are a predetermined number of warp threads in every 25 mm (1 in) of all fabrics. These are controlled by the nails in a rug or tapestry frame, by the thickness of the yarn in card and inkle loom weaving, by the slots and holes in a rigid heddle reed and by the reed of a loom with four or more shafts. The warp threads are held taut from both ends while weaving. The weft is passed across the warp between selected threads with a needle, stick shuttle or roller shuttle. A pick up stick can be used to form the space, called a shed, between warp threads through which the weft is passed. The weft is beaten down to form a right angle across the warp.

Use these projects to discover the basic principles and techniques of weaving. You can then experiment further to develop your skill and ideas and make your own discoveries. What is most important is to enjoy working with threads, to have fun dyeing yarn and the satisfaction of creating an original idea.

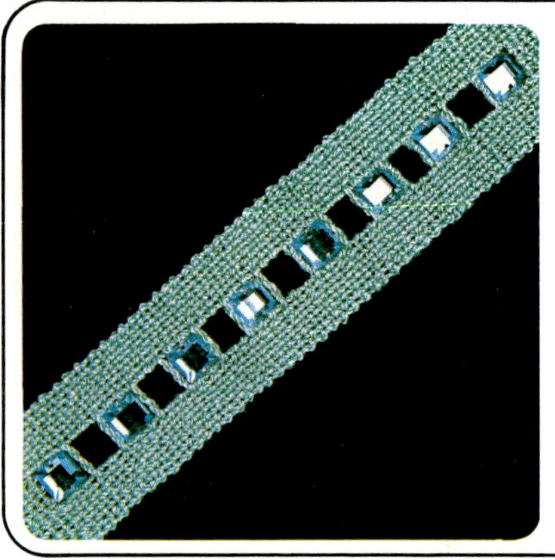

Needle Weaving

WOVEN NECKLACE

You will need:
Insulating board or plywood.
Large blunt needle
Pins
Yarn

Many useful and decorative objects can be woven without tools. The thread should be reasonably smooth and strong for the warp, but any type of yarn can be used for the weft, a tightly spun crochet yarn, corded rayon thread, metal thread or strips of polythene for example.

Make a rough drawing of your idea on paper before you begin. Dress patterns make good guides to the shape and size of things to wear.

Place the pins along the top and bottom edges of your design (1). Do not wind the threads too tightly round the pins since there is some take-up of the warp threads during weaving (2). When weaving bands it is best to use an even number of warp threads. For six threads you will have four pins at the top and three at the bottom of each band (1). Weave with a large needle (3). After pulling the weft thread

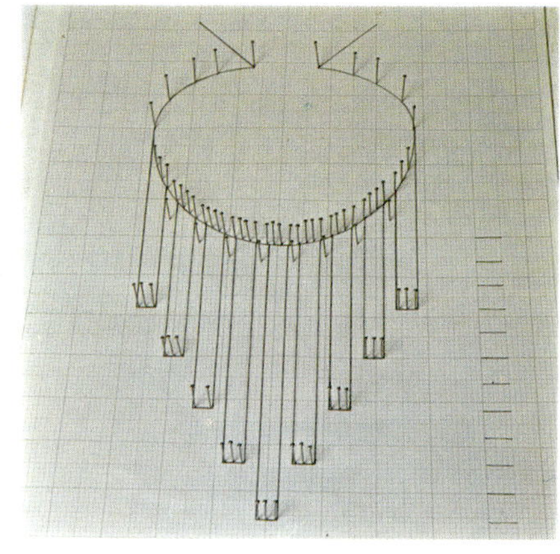

1 Fix pins securely along the top and bottom of your sketch making sure they stand straight.

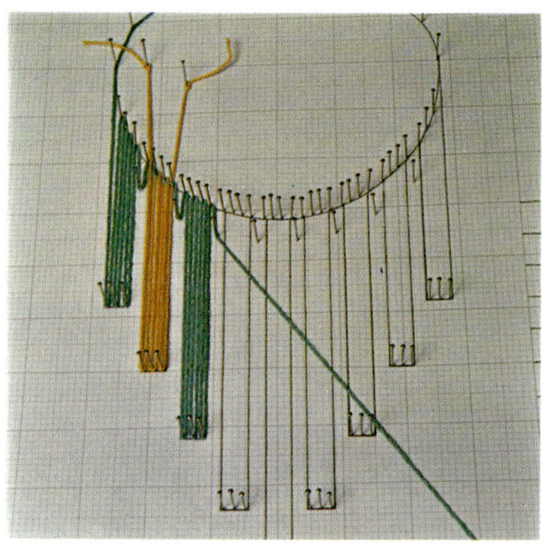

2 Secure the end of the thread to the board with a pin and wind the thread round the pins.

3 Pick up alternate threads with a needle and pull the weft across the warp and the space.

4 To secure the thread across the space twist the weft round it with your needle.

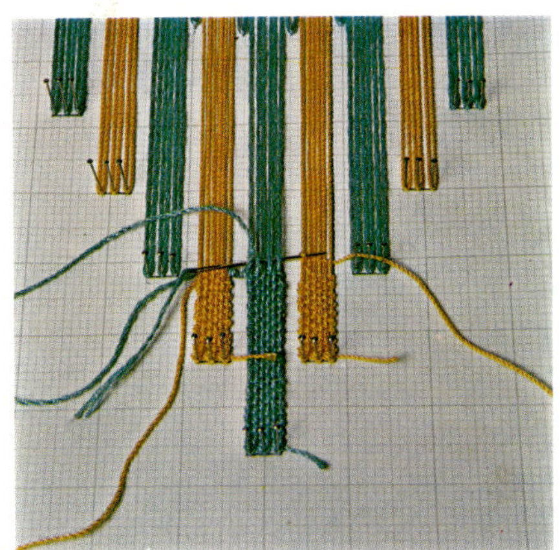

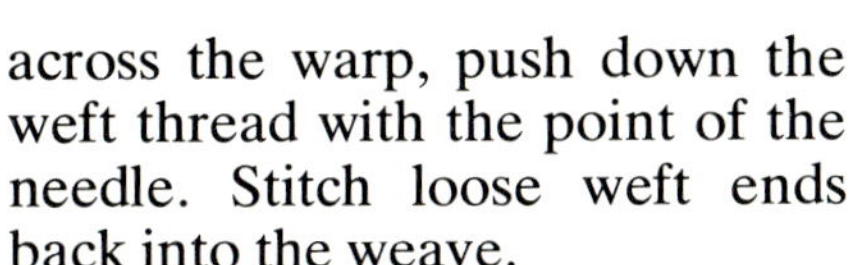

5 Pick up alternate threads and pull the weft across one section of the warp.

6 Make sure every loose end is stitched back or knotted before removing your object from the board.

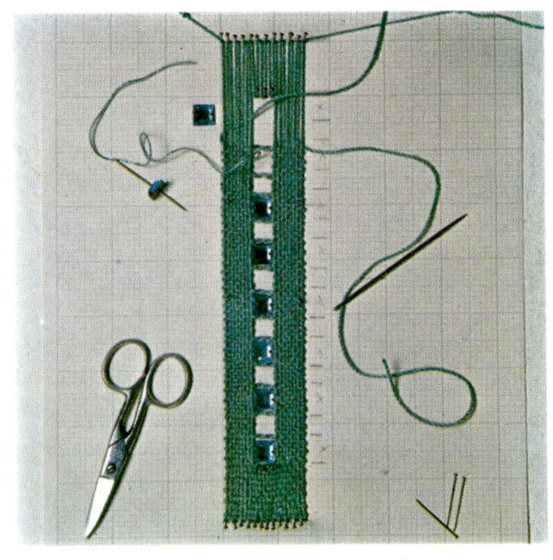

7 Fix beads by weaving a thin thread alongside one of the other wefts across the warp.

across the warp, push down the weft thread with the point of the needle. Stitch loose weft ends back into the weave.

Most jewelry looks more interesting if the design includes some areas of empty space. The threads across the space should be secure and stiff enough to support the shape of the piece (4). When knots occur in the construction, see if you can use them as an element of decoration, or as part of the fastening.

You may wish to weave in other objects such as beads, fur, feathers or pieces of metal. It is best to weave rather than stitch these objects into your fabric, or to suspend them on a thread which is woven into the structure.

Now make some other decorations and accessories such as the beaded bracelet shown here.

The bracelet is made of the same yarn as the necklace. Mark out the required pattern of the bracelet on the board, then using twelve pins at the top and bottom, and three pins 25 mm (1 in) from each end of the bracelet, wind on the warp threads. Weave the weft leaving spaces for the beads as shown in **7**. Use extra lengths of yarn to make a fastening.

Box Weaving

TABLE MATS

You will need:
Wooden box
Nails
Raffia
Flat sticks
Pick up stick
Stick shuttle
Blunt needle

Make or ask your grocer for a wooden box. Sandpaper the edges. Make marks 10 mm (⅜ in) apart along the two ends of your box. You will need one nail for every four warp threads. The number of warp threads per 25 mm (1 in) will depend on the thickness of the raffia. Eight or ten threads is recommended. Hammer the nails into the ends of the box by the marks, staggering them to avoid splitting the wood.

Hang up the bundle of raffia and pull strands from it to make the warp. Join the ends of the raffia by knotting them together as close to the nails as possible (1).

Start your table mat by weaving two flat sticks across the warp to allow extra warp for the fringe and to give a firm edge against which to weave (3).

1 Wind double threads of raffia backwards and forwards across your box between the nails.

2 Thread a lease stick carefully through the warp picking up alternate single threads of raffia.

3 Turn the lease stick on edge and pass the raffia weft through the space with the stick shuttle.

4 Thread the pick up stick through alternate warp threads coming from under the lease stick.

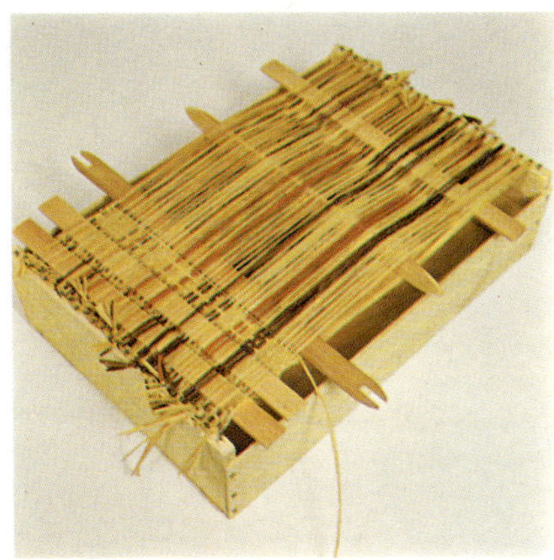

5 Turn the pick up stick on edge, pass the weft through the space, and beat down the weft.

6 To finish pass a needle under two weft threads from top to bottom with the loose end above the needle.

7 Then pass the needle behind the next two warp threads from right to left with loose end below needle.

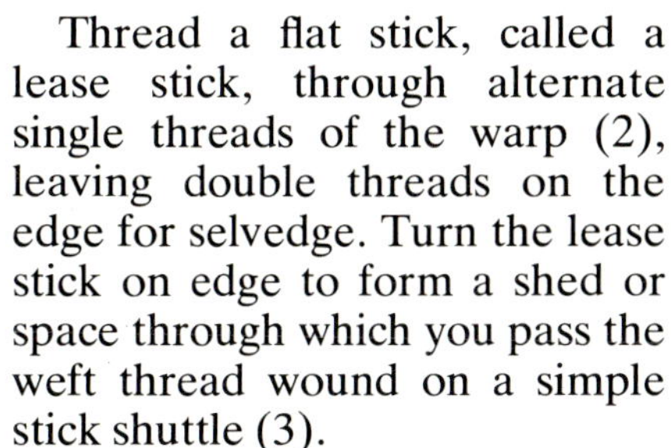

Thread a flat stick, called a lease stick, through alternate single threads of the warp (2), leaving double threads on the edge for selvedge. Turn the lease stick on edge to form a shed or space through which you pass the weft thread wound on a simple stick shuttle (3).

Pull the weft across the warp (3). Insert another flat stick with a pointed end, called the pick up stick, through the warp for the next weft thread (4). Turn the pick up stick on edge to make a shed and pass the weft thread through the space (5). Then push the weft down with the stick shuttle or lease stick (5). Try to keep the upper edge of the weft as even as possible. Do not pull the weft too tight. Continue to weave the weft across and back through alternate threads of the warp.

Stitch the ends of the mat while it is still on the box (6 and 7). Cut the mat off the box and trim the fringe with scissors.

Raffia can be dyed with household dyes. Table mats and small bags made of string, cotton or wool can be woven in this way, and a variety of woven squares can be stitched together to make a larger object.

Picture Weaving

You will need:
Beading wood or 25 × 25 mm
(1 × 1in) timber (thicker
wood for larger frames)
Glue
Frame clamp
Panel pins
Tenon saw
Mitre box
Thread

Making a frame
Decide on the size of your frame,
then measure and mark off your
wood. Cut the four sides with
each end at a 45° angle to make a
neat joint (1) at each corner.

If you are using beading wood
make sure that you cut the wood
in the right direction to join correctly at the corners of the frame.
You will inevitably waste a few
inches. Square wood can be
turned over after it has been cut
and be joined leaving no waste.

Glue the ends of each piece of
wood and assemble them exactly
at right angles on a table or board.
Hold the frame firmly in position
with a frame clamp and leave it
secured until the glue is dry (2).
Then drill through the corners at
the top and bottom of the frame
and hammer a panel pin into each
hole (3).

1 Hold or clamp the wood firmly
across the mitre block and cut with a
tenon saw.

2 Assemble your frame in the clamp
and slowly wind the handle to make
the wire taut.

3 Gently hammer a panel pin into
each hole at the top and bottom
corners of your frame.

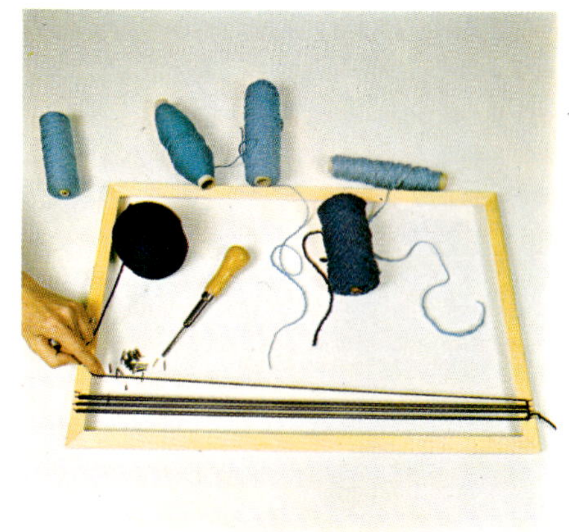

4 Wind the threads backwards and
forwards between the panel pins
across the frame in any direction.

Weaving pictures

Woven pictures should not be taken too seriously, and can be made in a day or an evening to be enjoyed, studied, admired, and then cut out of the frame and a new one made.

Weaving pictures is an excellent way to consider design, shape, space, colour, the character of different types of yarn, and even three dimensional form.

Any type of material can be used and it is a good idea to see what your local hardware store, electrical shop or rubbish dump can offer you. Start collecting string, ribbons, rags, washers, springs, and tubes made of paper, plastic or metal.

For inspiration it can help to have a subject in mind to start with, such as outer space, a landscape, rain, reflections, buildings, Christmas or a flower.

Oddments of smooth and textured blue wool threads and fine yellow wool and rayon threads have been used to make this picture (7).

Work from the back of the frame putting panel pins into the wood as you wind your threads backwards and forwards (4).

The straight lines of the threads across the frame can now be distorted by pulling them with threads from the side of the frame (5).

Wind fine yellow threads into a small hank which is even at one end and uneven at the other. Tie the threads tightly at the even end and cut them at the uneven end. Suspend them on a thread between the pins on the frame fixing them in position with a stitch (6).

The weaving on the right shows coloured drinking straws threaded on rayon threads woven across each other between the straws.

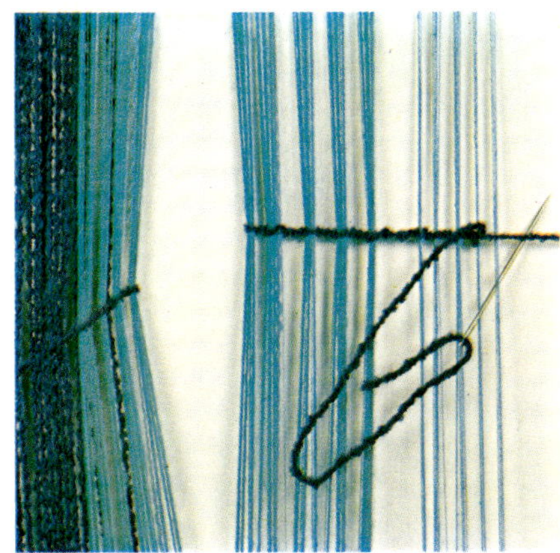

5 To weave or interlace the threads you will need to use a needle.

6 Attach a thread to the top of the frame and stitch it through the yellow threads.

7 To paint the frame, turn picture over and protect the threads at the edge with paper beforehand.

8 Shades of green and brown rayon threaded through wooden shuttle spools from the textile industry.

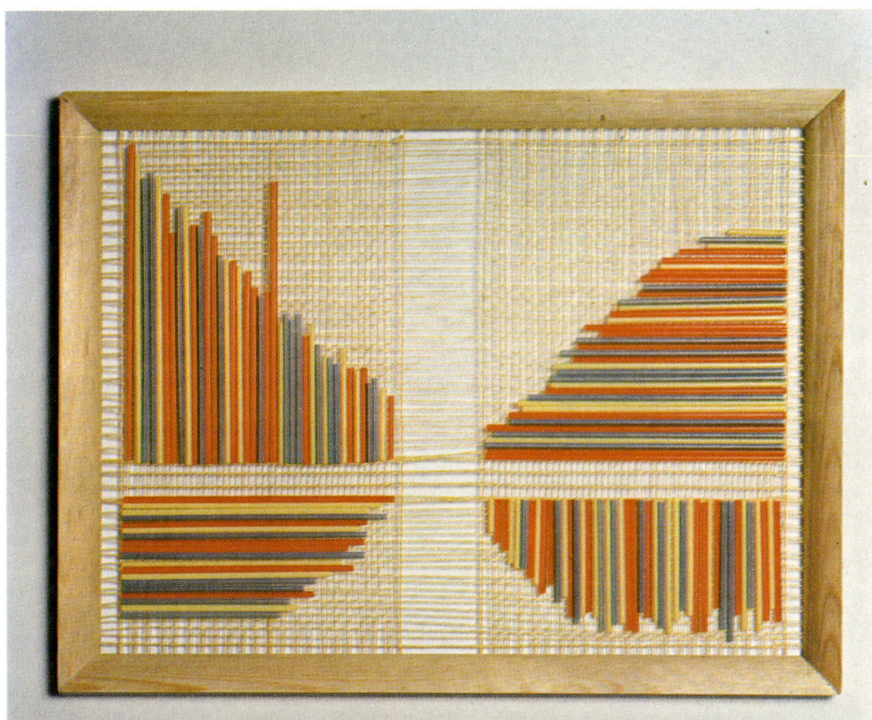

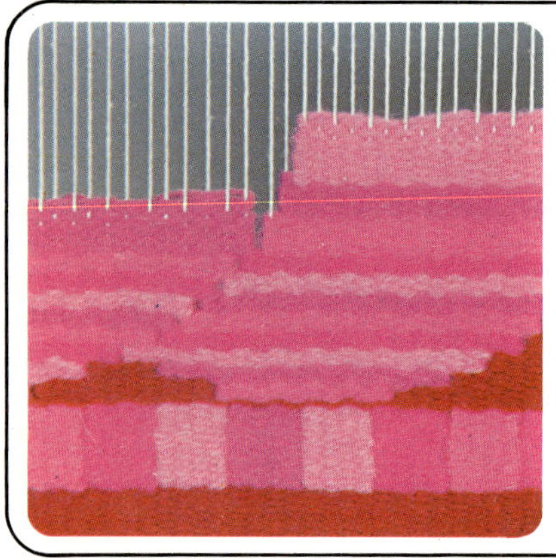

Tapestry Weaving

You will need:

Wood 25 × 25 mm (1 × 1 in) or
25 × 50 mm (2 × 1 in)
Tenon saw
Vice
Chisel
File or rasp
Two dresser hooks
Screws or nuts and bolts
Nails
Flat sticks
Suitable yarns

Frame

Decide on the size of your tapestry, and calculate the inside measurement of the frame, allowing an extra 100 mm (4 in) at the beginning, 380 mm (15 in) at the end and 25 mm (1 in) at each side. The extra length is allowed to enable you to separate the threads when weaving the last part of your tapestry.

Cut four lengths of wood for the four sides of the frame. Mark off the width of the wood at each end of the four pieces and cut at 90° to a depth of one third of the wood (1). Clamp each length of wood in a vice and chisel off the ends (1). Level the chiselled surface with a rasp or file.

Assemble your frame and drill holes in each corner for screws or

1 Clamp each piece of wood in the vice and chisel off one third of the total depth.

2 Assemble the frame and place screws in the holes already drilled in each corner.

3 Hammer in the nails, staggering them to prevent the wood from splitting.

4 Screw the length of wood, with the dresser hook attached, 150 mm (6 in) from the top of the frame.

nuts and bolts. Screw the frame together (2).

Make marks 10 mm (³⁄₈ in) apart along the top and bottom of the frame for nails. Add one extra mark on each side for selvedge. Hammer in the nails (3).

Cut two extra pieces of wood 125 mm (5 in) long, each with one end chiselled off as above (1). Screw dresser hooks into the other ends about 12 mm (½ in) from the tops (4), and screw the two pieces of wood to each side of the frame (4).

Wind the warp across the frame between the first two nails four or six times to make a selvedge thread (5). Complete the warp with four or six threads between the last two nails to make a selvedge on the other side of the tapestry.

Thread the lease stick across the warp (6).

Rest a rod on the dresser hooks across the frame (7). Tie the leash threads from the rod round alternate warp threads from under the lease stick and back to the rod. Use a continuous length of thread knotting it round the rod to prevent the leashes from slipping (7). Try to make sure that the leashes are the same length.

TAPESTRY

This tapestry is 400 × 320 mm (15¾ × 12½ in). The warp is made of strong four ply cotton. The weft is two ply carpet wool for the figure and three ply worsted for the background.

Turn the lease stick on edge and insert a stick through the space in the warp. Push this stick to the bottom of the frame to make a firm edge against which to weave.

Prepare your weft yarn by making butterflies of each colour (see Card Weaving page 20). Make a

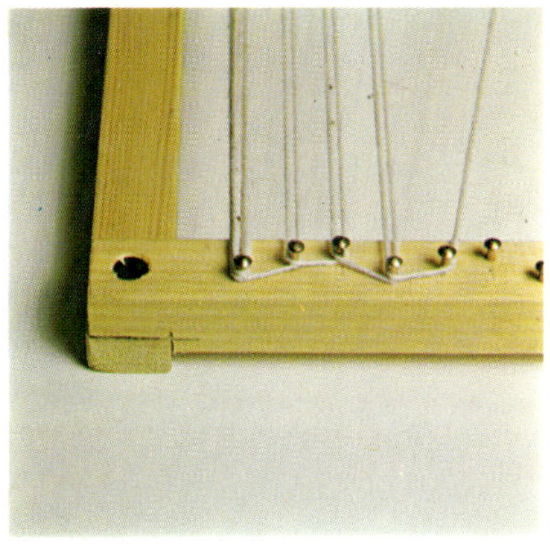

5 Wind threads across the frame round the nails at one end and across the nails at the other end.

7 Tie leash threads from the rod round alternate warp threads and back to the rod.

9 Turn the lease stick on edge and pass the weft through the space.

6 Thread a lease stick alternately in and out of the warp threads above the dresser hooks.

8 Pull a section of the leashes up with your fingers and pass the weft thread through the space.

10 Make a double turn with the weft round the last thread of the warp when required.

butterfly of your warp cotton using four strands together.

Unless you wish to finish by knotting the loose ends of the warp (see Rug Weaving page 29), weave 25 mm (1 in) of cotton at each end to give your tapestry a firm edge to hem.

Pull the leash threads towards you (8) and pass the weft through the space. Push the weft down with your fingertips. Turn the lease stick on edge (9) and pass the weft back through the space. Repeat these movements to weave. When weaving on a frame the edge of the fabric has a strong tendency to pull inwards. To prevent this encourage the fabric to pull slightly inwards for the first 25 mm (1 in). Now keep the fabric straight by weaving the weft loosely across the warp (11) to allow for the natural take up of the weft as it is pushed down.

Make a double turn round the selvedge thread when necessary, to keep a firm straight edge on the tapestry (10). Keep the warp tight. If necessary place a length of wood under the warp at the top of the frame.

If your design consists mainly of colour changes in vertical lines, you should weave your tapestry sideways unless you wish to make the slits part of your design. If you have only a few long vertical slits, these can be invisibly stitched together from the back of the tapestry with sewing thread. Short slits can be left (14).

When weaving refer frequently to your drawing (13). For large tapestries, using your drawing, draw the main outline of your design on the warp threads.

If your design has circular or diamond shapes it is easier to weave a section at a time but be sure that the first section you weave decreases in size or you will not be able to fill in the second

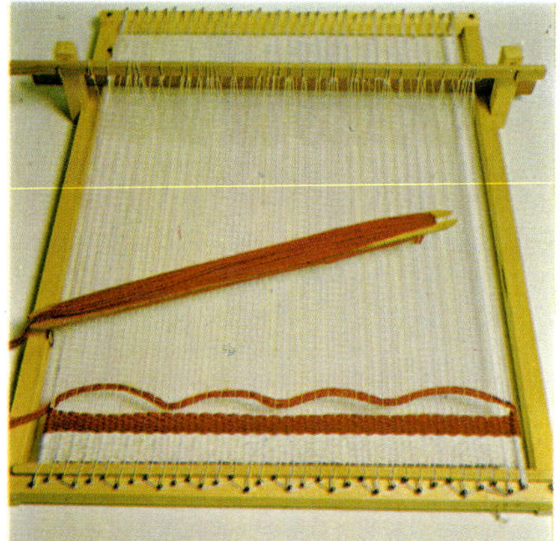

11 Keep the weft firm on the edge but loose across the warp before you push it down.

12 Join the yarn by separating each end through a different space in the warp and overlapping the ends.

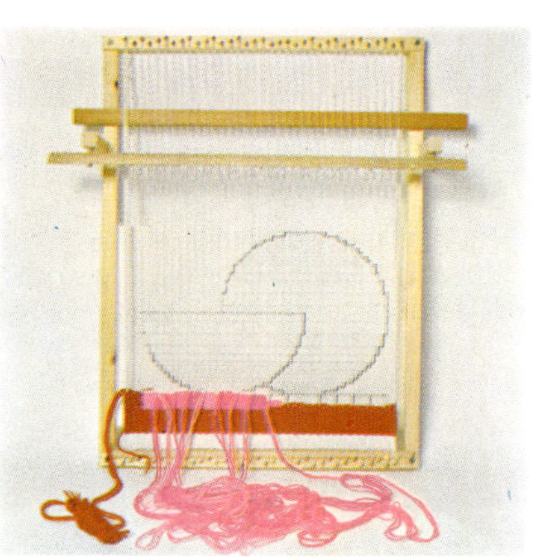

13 At intervals hold your drawing against your tapestry to check that you are weaving accurately.

14 To make vertical lines, change the colour between the warp threads leaving a slit in the fabric.

15 The first section woven must decrease in size whether it is on the edge or centre of your tapestry.

16 Start and end a colour in horizontal lines by weaving loose ends across two warp threads and back.

16

shape (15 and 17).

Interesting curved shapes can be made by weaving a bump in one colour and then weaving another colour across the whole warp allowing this weft to stretch right across the bump. Small sections left unwoven can also add interest to a tapestry.

Finish by hemming the cotton fabric you have woven at the top and bottom of your tapestry.

Cut the tapestry off the frame and trim back the warp threads to 12 mm (½ in). Press back the cotton fabric and hem down to the back of the tapestry (18).

17 The second section woven must increase in size to fit between the shapes woven in the first section.

18 The back of the finished tapestry, showing the woven cotton edge turned over and hemmed down.

Card Weaving

WOVEN BELT

You will need:
Set of 18 weaving cards
2 G-cramps (C-clamps)
Smooth stick or weaving shuttle
132 m (144 yds) or 150 g (5 oz) four ply worsted in 3 shades of blue
Belt fastener.

You can buy cards from a weaving equipment supplier or you can make your own with very stiff card and a punch for making the holes. If making the cards you will find it useful to mark one corner of each. The cards should be about 80 × 80 mm (3¼ × 3¼ in) with the centre of the holes about 15 mm (⅜ in) from the edge of the card at each corner. Slightly round off the corners. Alternatively, buy a pack of plastic playing cards, cut each card to a square and punch or burn out holes with a soldering iron.

Work along the edge of a flat surface, like a table; a length of wood is ideal, for easy storage. Any type of yarn which is strong and smooth is suitable.

Before you start it is advisable to weave a small test sample. This will help you to make the neces-sary calculations. It is suggested that a beginner start with a simple design of not more than two or three colours.

When you have decided what you are going to make, calculate the number and length of threads to be cut for the warp. Allow 300 mm (12 in) at the beginning and at least 460 mm (18 in) at the end of the warp for waste.

The belt illustrated is 860 mm (34 in) long and 65 mm (2½ in) wide.

Set the G-cramps 1.8 m (2 yds) apart for the warp. You will need 72 thick four ply worsted threads for the warp. Put blocks of wood under the G-cramps to make more space when weaving (1).

Wind 36 dark blue, 12 medium blue and 24 light blue threads round the G-cramps for the warp (1). Cut the warp threads and plait them loosely together (2).

The pattern in card weaving is achieved by the change of colour sequence through the four holes of the card. Simple card woven bands give a warp faced fabric and the weft plays no part in the design. The width of the band depends on the thickness of the yarn and the number of cards used, and is limited only by the number of cards you can control with your hands (8).

Thread card 1 by pulling four dark blue threads from the plait and threading one through each hole in the card. Thread from the back of the card to the front (3).

Thread card 2 the same way.

Thread cards 3 to 6 with one dark blue through one hole and three light blue threads through the other three holes in each card (4). Place the dark blue thread in a different hole for each card in the order of 1, 2, 3 and 4 (see threading draft).

Tie the first six cards together and place them flat on the table. Some patterns are threaded with the threads facing the same way throughout the cards. This belt is designed to have the threads facing the opposite way on one section, as shown by the arrows on the threading draft.

Thread card 7 with four dark blue threads and cards 8 to 11 with one dark blue thread through one hole and three medium blue threads through three holes in each card (5).

Remember this time to thread from the front of the card to the back and reverse the order of the dark blue threads to 4, 3, 2 and 1

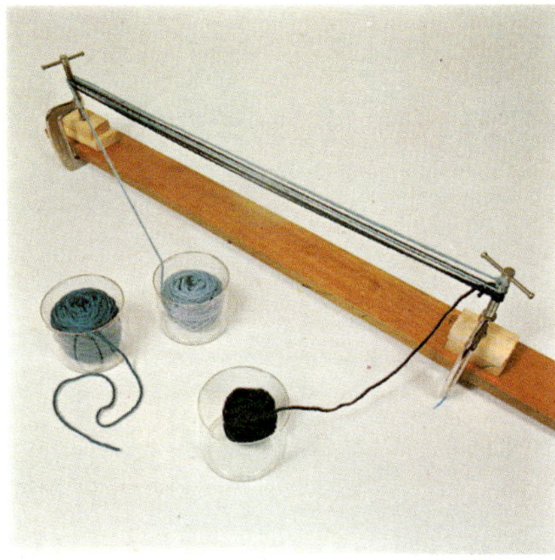

1 Wind the worsted round the clamps until enough threads have been made in each colour.

2 Cut the threads at either end by the clamp. Plait these threads loosely together.

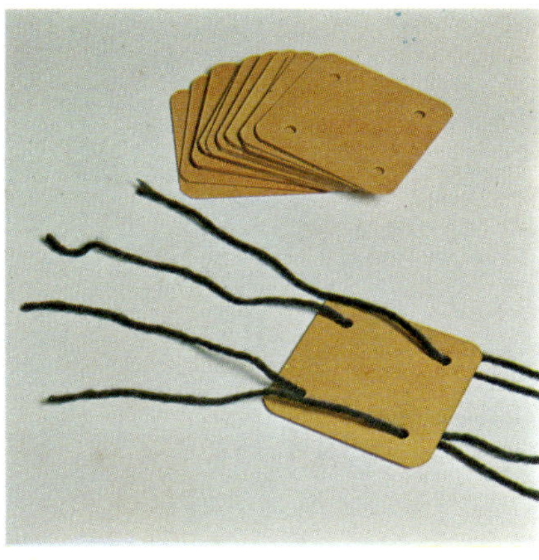

3 Pull four dark threads from the plait and thread one through each hole of card 1.

(see threading draft).

Thread card 12 with four dark blue threads and tie these six cards together. Cards 13 to 16 are threaded in the same direction as cards 3 to 6. Cards 17 and 18 are threaded in the same way as cards 1 and 2.

Tie all three sections of cards together. Tie all the threads at the front end of the warp together with an overhand knot. Divide the warp threads and pass them over the G-cramp (6). Hold the back of the warp and pull the threads to obtain an even tension. Divide the threads and tie them round the other G-cramp in a half bow (6).

Untie the cards. Check that the dark blue thread on each card corresponds with the threading draft. Divide the warp in half and using two butterflies of prepared weft yarn (7) weave two bands separately for 100 mm (4 in) as supports for the ring fasteners. End one of the weft yarns by overlapping it with the other weft. Weave across the complete warp with the remaining weft.

When weaving keep the cards about 150 mm (6 in) from the edges of the fabric. Pass the weft through the space and pull it tightly across the warp. Push the weft down firmly with a smooth stick or shuttle before turning the cards (9).

Turn the cards forward in a clockwise direction (8), and weave until you have completed 12 wefts. Now turn the cards backwards and anti-clockwise and weave for another 12 wefts. See from the finished belt on page 19 where the pattern changes direction. When you have woven 600 mm (24 in) of the belt, divide the warp in the centre and using two wefts weave two separate bands for the fastening at the end of the belt. To taper the ends of

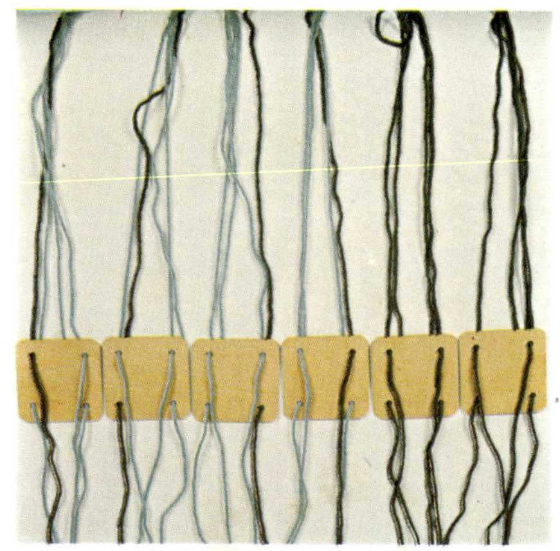

4 Thread cards 1 to 6 with the warp threaded through the holes from back to front of each card.

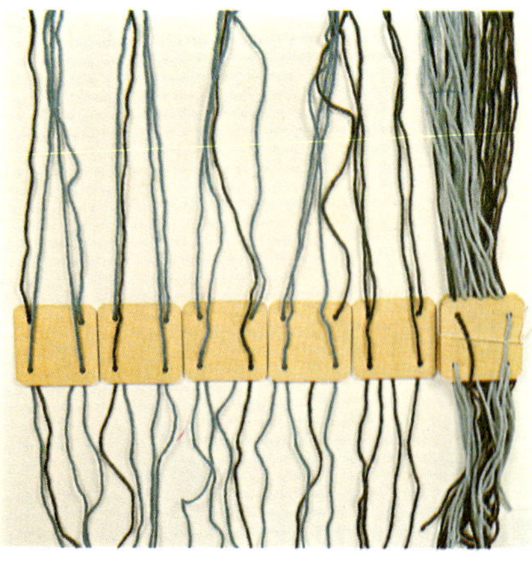

5 Thread cards 7 to 11 with the warp threaded through the holes from front to back of each card.

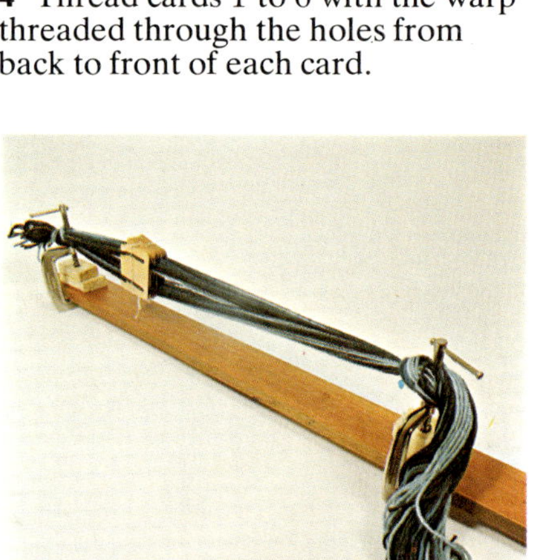

6 Warp held under tension round clamps with cards tied together until you are ready to weave.

7 Prepare the weft by winding the yarn into a butterfly, and wrapping some yarn round the centre.

8 Grasp all the cards with both hands and turn them forward in a clockwise direction.

9 Push the weft down firmly with a smooth stick before turning the cards for the next weft thread.

Cards

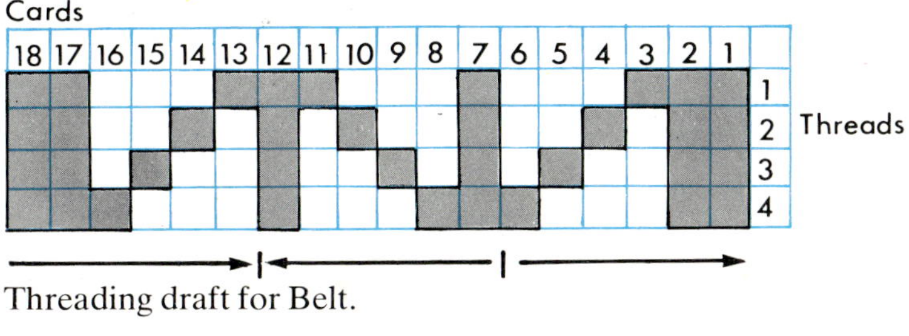

Threading draft for Belt.

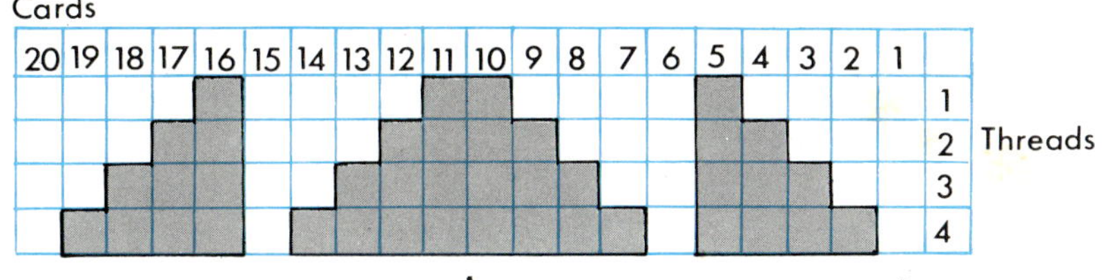

Threading draft for Wall Hanging.

these bands, cut the edge thread of the warp and weave it across as weft, first from the right of the band and then from the left. Tie an overhand knot in the remaining warp threads.

WALL HANGING

You will need:
660 m (720 yds) or 500 g (17 oz) four ply worsted in six colours
60 weaving cards
18 wooden rods 350 mm (14 in) long
4 G-cramps (C-clamps)

The hanging is 2 m (6½ ft) long and 300 mm (12 in) wide, made with three bands of weaving, each requiring 80 threads and 20 cards.

Make the warp 2.75 m (9 ft) long.

Thread the cards with the darkest threads as indicated in the threading draft. Note that each section of ten cards is threaded in opposite directions as shown by the arrows in the draft.

Attach two G-cramps 140 mm (5½ in) apart at each end of a board or table. Tie one end of the warp to a stick resting across the G-cramps and tension the other end of the warp to a stick across the G-cramps at the opposite end of the board.

Weave in opposite directions between the rods by turning the cards clockwise, inserting a rod, and turning the cards anti-clockwise. The rods can be tightly woven into the fabric by making an extra turn of the cards, without a weft thread, before and after inserting the rod.

For plain sections weave twelve weft threads before inserting the rod. For small crossed sections weave an extra four weft threads on the two narrow bands. On the sections where the threads cross the space weave twenty threads across and an extra four on the two crossing narrow bands.

Each time you change the position of the cards groups of threads cross in the warp. Keep this crossing to the back of the warp by placing a few sticks alternatively over and under each band (eventually you will need to undo the warp and put it in order). As you weave, roll the fabric up, tie it round tightly with string and replace it across the G-cramps.

Weave an extra 50 mm (2 in) at the beginning and at the end to turn back around the first and last rods for a neat finish.

Inkle Loom Weaving

There are two types of inkle loom; a small and conveniently portable table model, which will make bands up to 2 m (2¼ yds) long, and a floor model which is a substantial loom for making longer bands.

You can make a wooden table model for yourself with an elementary knowledge of carpentry.

The leashes are loops made of a fine strong cotton cord or heddle string.

Bands made on an inkle loom are warp faced fabrics with the weft hardly visible, so choose an attractive yarn for the warp.

The maximum width of band that can be woven on an inkle loom is about 100 mm (4 in), and various lengths are made by either including or missing out some of the pegs at the back of the loom.

The warp threads must always go round the front peg, across to the top peg at the back of the loom and round the adjustment peg whatever the length of the warp might be.

Always tie a warp thread to itself, never to a peg on the loom.

WEAVING A BAND

For the warp use alternate threads of thick and thin cotton at 28 threads per 25 mm (1 in).

Take the first warp thread from the front peg on the loom, round the other pegs, including the adjustment peg, and back to the front peg. Knot the end of this back on itself (3 and 4).

Wind the second warp thread in the same zig-zag direction as the first, but this time thread it through the loop of the first leash (5).

When making the warp be sure to keep the tension of the threads even. It is important that all the warp threads should be wound round the loom as a continuous thread (6).

Complete the warp by knotting the end of the last warp thread back on to itself. Prepare the weft yarn (7).

Press down on the leashes with one hand while raising the opposite threads of the warp with the shuttle to make a space through which the shuttle passes (10). Pull the weft tightly across the warp (9). Use the shuttle to push the weft threads down at right angles to the warp.

1 Simple table model of an inkle loom complete with leashes and a shuttle.

2 Warp tension adjustment peg held by a bolt and wing nut on the back of the loom.

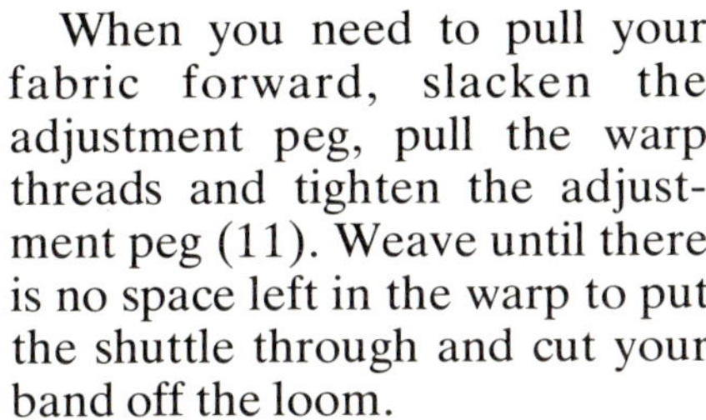

3 Take the first warp thread from peg on the left below next peg to peg at the top of the back of the loom.

4 Wind the warp thread zig-zag between pegs, including the adjustment peg, at the end of the frame.

5 Thread the second warp thread through the loop of the first leash to the right of the first thread.

When you need to pull your fabric forward, slacken the adjustment peg, pull the warp threads and tighten the adjustment peg (11). Weave until there is no space left in the warp to put the shuttle through and cut your band off the loom.

You can make a variety of bands in different widths and many different types of yarn on this simple inkle loom. For example, belts, straps, harnesses, bellpulls, ribbons and braids. Bands can also be stitched together to make aprons, bags and simple garments.

To make the shoulder bag illustrated, weave six bands 330 mm (13 in) long for the front and back, four bands 250 mm (10 in) long for the front, and one band 1.9 m (2 yds) long for the gusset and strap. All the bands are 75 mm (3 in) wide.

Weave seven bands across each other to make a decorative panel on the front of the bag, three lengthwise and the four shorter bands across, and stitch them together. Stitch three bands together lengthwise to make the back, and use one long band to make the gusset and strap.

OVEN GLOVE

You will need:
Inkle loom and shuttle
300 m (322 yds) or 150 g (5 oz)
thick cotton thread in three
colours

Weave two bands 1.1 m (44 in)
long and 90 mm (3½ in) wide.
Make the warp 1.5 m (5 ft) long
using 77 thick cotton threads at
24 threads per 25 mm (1 in). To
give a strong edge to the fabric
make a double warp thread on
each side. For the weft use a thick
white cotton.

To make a warp for this pattern
use two colours and white in the
following order:
9 brown;
2 white;
1 brown 1 white (twice);
2 brown 1 white 1 brown (twice);
2 white;
1 brown 1 white (three times);
4 white;
2 blue 1 white (three times);
2 blue;
4 white;
1 white 1 brown (six times);
2 brown 1 white (three times);
8 brown.

Consider using a fancy stitch to
join the two bands together.

You can produce a variety of
patterns by changing the colour or
order of colour in the warp. Warp
threads can be cut off and a
different coloured thread knotted
on to the ends of these threads
during the weaving. The knots
can be concealed at the back or
used as decoration on the front of
the fabric.

Cut the two finished bands off
the loom and join them together
lengthwise. At each end turn in
the raw ends 25 mm (1 in) and
hem. Turn in a further 160 mm
(6 in), pad with cotton sheeting
and sew up the sides to make the
pockets.

6 After completing one stripe
change colour by knotting the new
thread to the old.

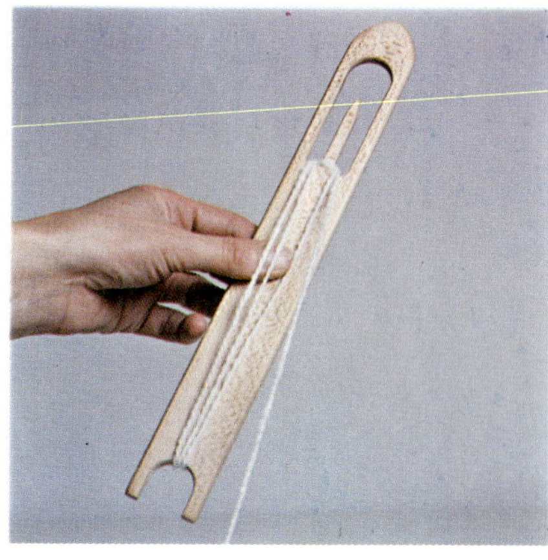

7 Wind the weft yarn on to the
shuttle changing direction round the
spike at the pointed end.

8 Pass the shuttle through the space
between the upper and lower layers
of the warp.

9 Pull weft tightly across the warp
controlling edge of the fabric with the
fingers of the other hand.

10 Maintain space for the shuttle
with the thumb while the fingers of
the left hand press down leashes.

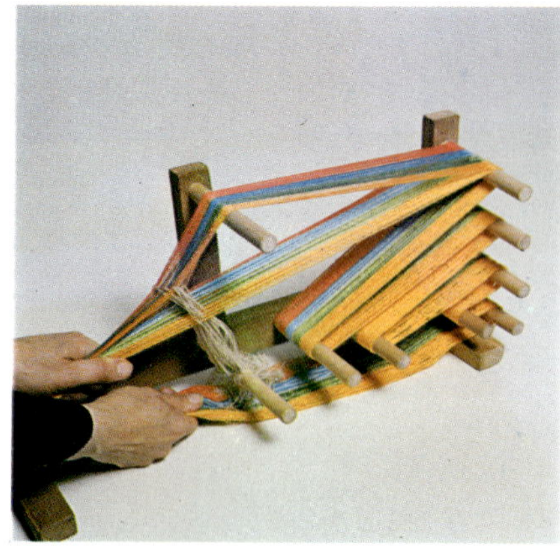

11 Slacken the adjustment peg, and
grasp the warp in both hands to pull
the fabric forward.

Rug Weaving

WOOL RUG

You will need:
Frame at least 0.75 × 1.8 m
(2½ × 6 ft)
Nails for frame
Four bolts and wing nuts
Strong plied cotton for warp
2 k (4 lb) two ply carpet yarn
Rug beater
Lease and pick up sticks
Stick shuttle

The advantage of weaving on a rug frame is that it can be leant against the wall and takes up little space.

The frame can be made of wood to the dimensions above for most rug work of moderate size. Join the corners of wood cut to size with bolts and wing nuts for easy assembly and storage. Use timber not less than 25 × 50 mm (2 × 1 in) for strength.

You can equally well use an old single bed frame but, if metal, batten timber to each end to hold nails for warp threads.

Warping the frame
Hammer nails 16 mm (⅝ in) apart along each end of the frame to a width of 740 mm (29 in). This allows 25 mm (1 in) each side for

1 Rug frame showing lease stick suspended from top of frame and leashes knotted in groups of five.

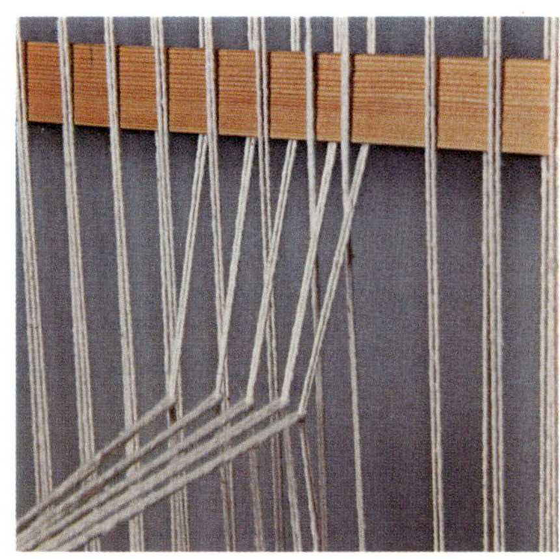

2 Pull a group of leashes forward with your hand to pass the weft through the space.

3 Two wefts of dark across one section of warp and two wefts of light across the other section.

4 Two light threads woven across both sections of warp. Carry dark thread behind for next dark weft.

the pulling in of the edge while weaving.

Wind a double thread of strong plied cotton tightly across the frame to make the warp, with four double threads on each side for selvedge.

Weave a lease stick through alternate double warp threads and suspend it with a cotton thread about 600 mm (24 in) from the top of the frame. Make leashes below the lease stick with the cotton warp used single. Pass 250 mm (10 in) lengths of single warp cotton round alternate warp threads below and at the back of the lease stick. Tie groups of five strands of cotton together with an overhand knot to form leashes (1).

Weaving

The rug is 690 × 1320 mm (27 × 52 in), made with six colours, five tones of brown and a bleached white. Four strands of two ply carpet yarn cover the warp easily and give a more interesting textural surface than a thick rug yarn. If your weft does not completely cover the warp, the weft is either too thick or pulled too tightly across the warp.

Stand the frame on a chair or stool protected by a rubber mat to prevent it from slipping: this gives a comfortable working height to start, and you can lower the frame to the floor as work progresses.

Weave a few flat sticks across the frame to give a firm edge against which to weave and to leave enough warp at the end of the rug for knotting.

The weft is made into a butterfly or wound on to a stick shuttle.

To weave the pattern, pull a group of leashes forward (2) and pass the weft through the space.

Turn the lease stick on edge and pass the weft through the

5 Two wefts of dark thread across one section of the warp followed by one weft of light thread.

6 Pick up the dark weft yarn which was left on the front of the rug and weave two weft threads.

7 To make vertical lines in the design weave alternate coloured weft threads.

8 Twist the weft threads round each other to prevent the end warp thread from remaining uncovered.

9 Pass a length of weft yarn over two warp threads and behind one keeping the loop above the thread.

10 Pass a length of weft yarn over two warp threads and behind one keeping the loop below the thread.

space. Push the weft down using the tips of your fingers, a rug beater or a blunt tool such as a screw driver or a dinner fork.

Pull in the sides of your rug for the first 25 mm (1 in) of weaving, then keep the sides straight by weaving loosely to allow for the natural take up of the weft as it is pushed down.

As you work the pattern, join the weft weaving loose ends across two warp threads and back, and leaving the ends at the back of the frame to be trimmed later to 12 mm (½ in).

Two weft threads of one tone are followed by two of another. This makes horizontal lines. Continue this pattern for 27 mm (5 in) (3 and 4). Alternate tones of colour will make vertical lines (7).

Make small spots by using two wefts of a dark tone followed by one weft of a light, followed by two wefts of dark (6, 7, 8). Now try a slightly raised surface by adding weft stitching (9, 10, 11).

Make larger spots by using two dark, one light, one dark, one light and two dark threads (10, 11).

This is the basic pattern, continue until the carpet is the correct length. You can modify the design at will by any combination of the above patterns.

When you have completed your rug cut it off the frame and knot the ends of the warp (12, 13). Trim the ends of the weft on the back of the rug, having woven any loose ends across two warp threads and back.

Do not line the rug. Friction between the two surfaces destroys the back. Use one of the commercially produced non slip materials if necessary.

11 After each stitch is made pull the end of the thread down firmly to make an even row.

12 Take two warp threads and tie an overhand knot making sure the knot is firmly against the weft.

13 Your rug can be finished with one row of knots and the warp ends trimmed back 50 mm (2 in).

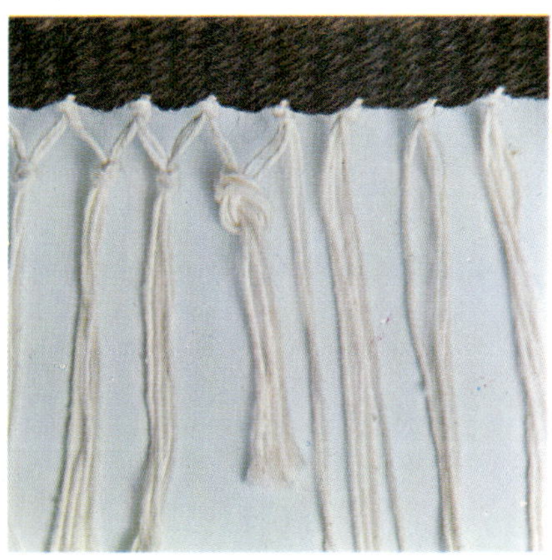

14 To make a decorative fringe take one warp thread from each knot and make a second row of knots.

SISAL DOOR MAT

You will need:
Rug frame
2 k (4 lb 4 oz) three ply sisal
Dyes (optional)
Scissors and comb
Stick shuttle
Pick up stick
Flat sticks

Make a rug frame adding 460 mm (18 in) to the chosen length of your mat for a fringe and warp wastage.

The mat illustrated is a large door mat 610 × 915 mm (24 × 36 in) including the fringe.

Use its natural colour, or dip dye about 1.5 k (3½ lb) of your sisal string for the warp and weft, and the rest a single colour for the rya knots (see Chemical Dyes page 62).

Sisal string is thick and springy and does not stretch so there is a considerable take up of the warp when weaving. Hammer nails into the ends at the outer edges of the frame 10 mm (⅜ in) apart for the warp. Tie a length of wood 25 × 50 mm (2 × 1 in) across the top and bottom of the frame to take up the slack (15). Use more sticks if necessary when you have wound on the warp. Remove these as the warp becomes too tight for weaving.

Wind the warp across the frame using a double thread for selvedge. Make a double turn round this when weaving.

Thread two sticks through alternate warp threads and push the sticks to the top of the frame (15). These keep the threads in order and help you select correctly with the pick-up stick.

Thread the pick up stick over two and under two warp threads (16), turn it on edge and pass the weft through the space. Push the weft down. Then thread the pick up stick over two and under two warp threads again, but this time moving one thread to the right of the previous pair (16).

Continue this method of pick up and you are weaving your mat in a two and two twill weave. Take care to keep the weft loose to prevent the warp from pulling in. Keep the weft pushed down with your finger tips or by hitting it with a rug beater.

Before making the rya knots, thread the pick up stick across the warp in preparation for the next twill weft.

Rya knots

The yarn for knots is not cut into individual lengths before knotting. It is taken from a large ball of yarn. Keep scissors permanently in the dominant hand to cut the knots.

To make a rya knot, take one end of the weft thread down between two warp threads, bring it round and up from behind outside one warp thread, over and across the top of the pair, down behind the second warp thread, and bring the end up through the centre where you started (18). Pull the knot down tightly and cut

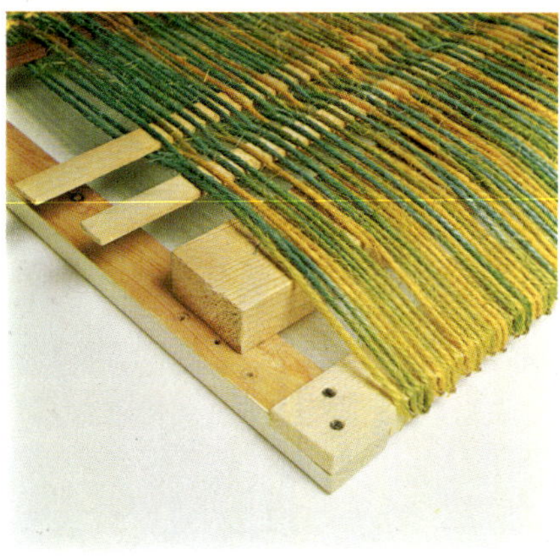

15 Rug frame showing lease sticks, tension bar and nails holding the warp on the edge of the frame.

16 Thread the pick up stick over two and under two warp threads for a two and two twill weave.

17 To join the weft, unravel the ply and push each end through a different space between the warps.

18 Push the weft down between two warp threads, round them and back up between them for rya knots.

19 Pull the rya knot down and adjusting the yarn to the required length, cut off the single end.

20 When you have completed a section of rya knots, comb the twist out of the sisal with a coarse comb.

the loose ends. The irregularity of hand-cut ends adds character to the weave.

To keep the selvedges straight, make an extra turn of weft instead of a knot at each side.

Weave two weft threads to keep the weaving level in place of any knots you may decide to leave out across the warp.

Finally, comb the twist out of the sisal in the rya knots (20), and oversew both ends of the mat (21). Cut the mat from the frame, trim the warp ends back to 50 mm (2 in), and comb the twist out of the fringe.

21 To finish, split the sisal and oversew with two ply thread across two warps and behind two wefts.

RAG RUG

You will need:
Rug frame
Cotton strips
Strong cotton thread for warp
Dye

This rug is 760 × 1320 mm (30 × 50 in) and is made from cotton fabric of various colours and designs, dyed with direct turquoise chemical dye (see Chemical Dyes page 61–63), then torn into strips 12 mm (½ in) wide and wound into balls ready for weaving.

22 Detail of blue rag rug. It is not always possible to cover the whole of the warp when weaving rags.

Some thick blue rug wool, left over from another project, is used in part of the rug.

Set the nails at each end of the frame 12 mm (½ in) apart for the warp. The warp is made of single strands of strong cotton, dyed turquoise blue, with extra threads on each side for the selvedge.

In rag rugs the warp threads are not usually completely covered by the weft (22).

Joins in the weft are made by overlapping the ends across four warp threads.

Now you can apply tapestry and rug weaving techniques to your own ideas for a rug. See what yarns you have left over from your weaving, and fabrics from dressmaking, or any unwanted clothes. Dying the material helps to co-ordinate the colour of the rug.

Try using tapestry techniques in a rag rug with an area of rya knots made with rags or try rya knots in a large tapestry woven on your rug frame; there are endless possibilities at your finger tips.

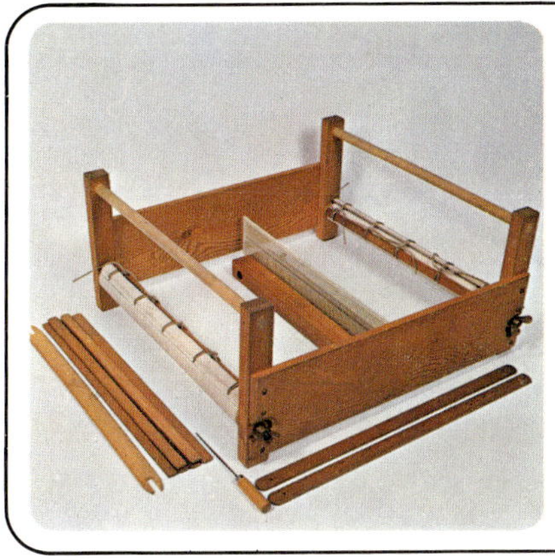

Rigid Heddle Loom

You will need:
Rigid heddle roller loom
Rigid heddle and wooden clamp
Warping board or posts
Warp sticks and two lease sticks
Small threading hook
Stick shuttle and pick up stick

Count the number of holes and slots per 25 mm (1 in) in the heddle to calculate the number of threads you will need for the warp. Heddles vary from five threads per 25 mm (1 in) for exceptionally coarse weaving with thick warp threads, to eight threads per 25 mm (1 in) as used to make the cushion covers, or twelve per 25 mm (1 in) as used for the table mats. The thread should be of a suitable size to slide easily through the slots and holes of the heddle.

Decide on the colour arrangement, width and length of your fabric, and make the warp allowing 460 mm (18 in) extra length for waste and double threads on each side for selvedge.

A warp is a given number of threads in a particular order made to a calculated length in preparation for winding round the roller on the loom. This is not a difficult operation if you work carefully

1 Two double warping posts, one pair clamped to the table with a small clamp.

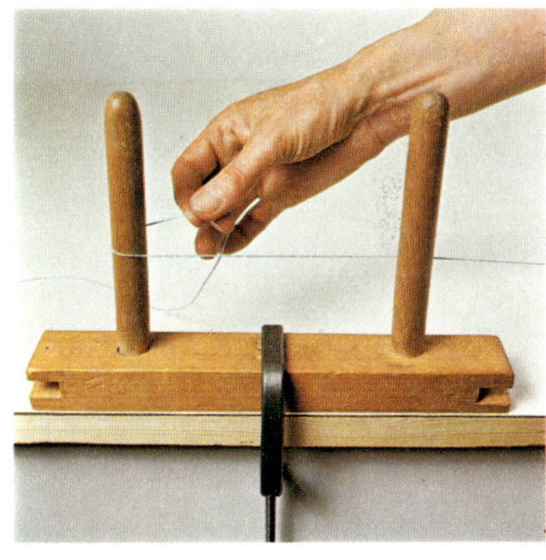

2 Take a length of thread and pass it behind one peg and in front of the other for the first warp thread.

3 Make a figure of eight between the two pegs for the second warp thread.

4 The figure of eight cross in the warp is made between the double posts at each end of the warp.

and methodically, and continuously check with the instructions to prevent mistakes.

You can buy, or with an elementary knowledge of carpentry, make your own warping posts for short warps of not more than 1.8 m (2 yds) (1). You may be able to adapt the up-turned legs of chairs, knife handles stuck in the ground, or four G-cramps.

You will need to make or buy a warping board for longer warps. This can also be used for short warps (see page 41).

To keep the warp threads in the correct positions for threading, a cross in the form of a figure of eight is made at each end of the warp (3, 4, 5).

TABLE MATS

You will need:
450 m (492 yds) or 100 g (3½ oz) of mercerised cotton thread
Rigid heddle roller loom and accessories

For three mercerised cotton table mats 260 × 380 mm (10¼ × 15 in) including the fringe, make the warp 1.6 m (5 ft 3 in) long.

Clamp the warping posts 1.6 m (5 ft 3 in) apart or measure this length between the pegs on the warping board. Tie the end of the first warp thread around the first peg on the right hand warping post and pass it behind the other peg. Take this first thread across the table behind one and in front of the other peg on the left hand warping post (2). Complete the lease or cross by taking the second warp thread behind one peg and in front of the other on the left hand warping post (3). Then take this thread across the table to complete the lease on the right hand warping post. Check that you are making a correct figure of eight cross round the pegs on each

5 Change the colour of the warp by knotting the threads together as near to the end peg as possible.

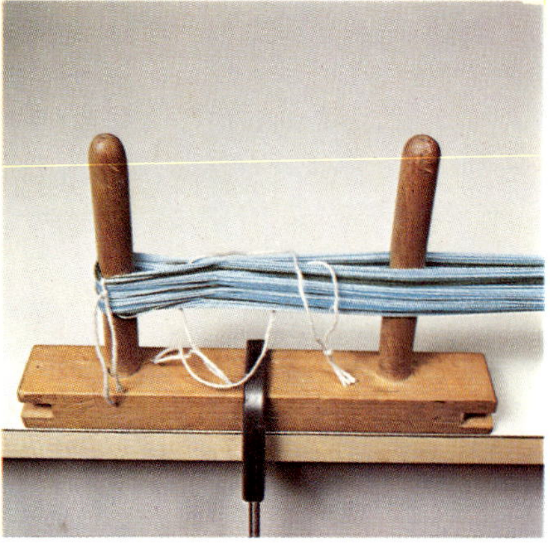

6 Tie the centre of the cross in the warp by taking a thread down by one peg and up by the other.

7 Separate the warp threads at the cross and put one cross stick through each space.

8 Thread the first loop of the warp through a slot in the rigid heddle and slip the warp stick through it.

9 Divide the cord round the warp stick and use it to tie the stick to the back roller with a square knot.

10 Hold the warp firmly at an even tension at the front of the loom to wind the warp on the roller.

of the two sets of posts (4).

Change the colour of the warp by knotting the two threads together. It is important that the warp should be made of a continuous thread (5). Always count the warp threads at the cross.

When you have completed the warp, make ties with strong thread of a different colour: tie the lease or cross at each end of the warp by taking a length of string down by one peg and up by the other, tie the ends of string together with an overhand knot (6); tie the loop at each end of the warp by the peg (6), and make a tight tie, with a bow, round the centre of the warp to hold all the warp threads together. Check that the warp is tied correctly.

Slacken the clamp on the left hand warping post. Grasp the warp with the end hanging down towards your elbow and wind the threads round your hand into a loose ball. Tuck the end of the warp, from the right hand warping post, under the wrapping of threads round the ball (9–10 page 42–44).

Hold the string tie on each side of the lease at the end of the warp, coming from the centre of the ball, to separate the warp threads. Put one lease stick through each space (7). Check that the lease sticks are correctly placed in the warp and tie them together at each end.

Remove the string tie from the cross. Place the heddle in the wooden clamp. Remove the warp stick from the roller at the back of the loom. Remove the tie round the loop at the end of the warp.

Each pair of warp threads crosses in a figure of eight round the lease sticks and is joined in a loop at the front.

Thread the first loop of the warp through a slot in the heddle with a threading hook, and slip

11 Place warp sticks under the warp at intervals when winding the warp on to the roller.

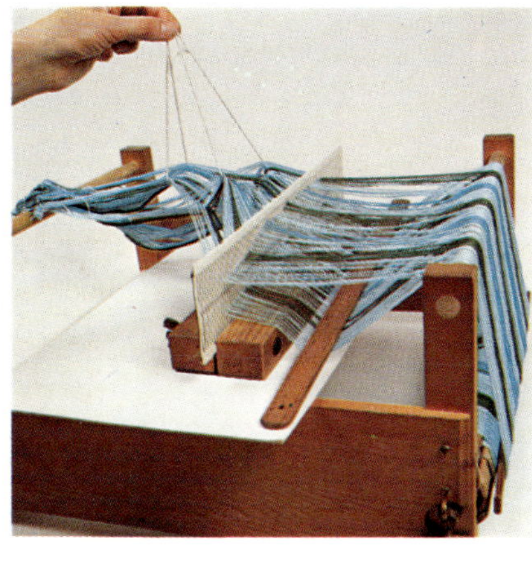

12 Separate the warp threads at the cross and put the first cross stick through the space.

13 Separate the warp threads at the cross and put the second cross stick through the space.

14 Thread warp threads which are over the nearest cross stick through the holes in the heddle.

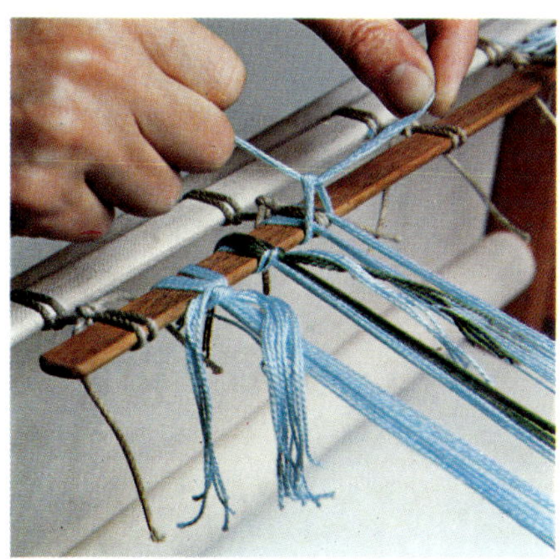

15 Tie groups of twelve threads round the stick at the front of loom and tie half the square knot.

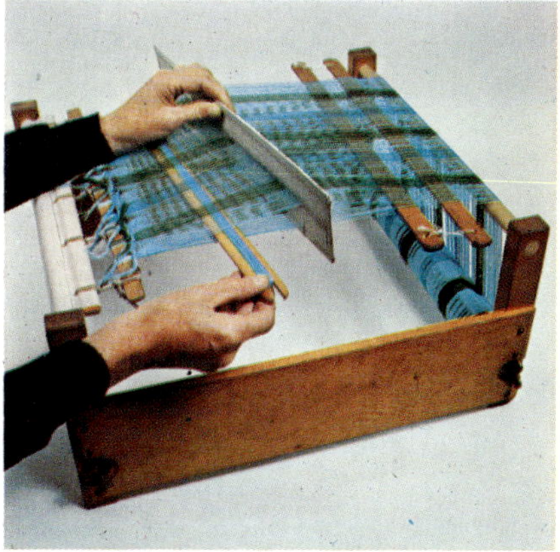

16 Lift the rigid heddle up and pass the shuttle through the space between the threads.

the stick from the warp roller through the loop (8). Continue to thread the pairs of warp threads through the slots in the heddle.

Place the clamp holding the rigid heddle in the loom. Tie the warp stick to the back roller of the loom (9).

Raise the heddle on a board placed across the loom under the clamp. Remove the lease sticks. Grasp the warp where the threads are tied together, hold it down resting across the front bar of the loom, and even out the tension of the threads. Turn the roller round four times to start winding on the warp. Cover with a warp stick any knots which may cause unevenness. Insert a layer of warp sticks round the roller under the warp threads placing each stick about 25 mm (1 in) apart (11). The layer of warp sticks is important because they prevent the edge threads falling off the wrappings of warp round the roller. If this happens these threads become shorter than the others and the edge of the fabric is too tight when weaving. If you do not have enough warp sticks a layer of stiff paper will do. Continue to wind the warp on to the loom with another four turns of the roller and insert more warp sticks until the cross at the end of the warp is 150 mm (6 in) from the heddle (12). Tie the end of the warp to the front bar of the loom. Hold the string tie at each side of the warp to separate the warp threads at the cross. Insert the first lease stick through the space at the back of the rigid heddle (12).

Carefully undo the tie through the cross in the warp and remove the string from the space in the half of the cross where you have put the lease stick. Tie together the ends of string which remain in the other half of the cross. Separ-

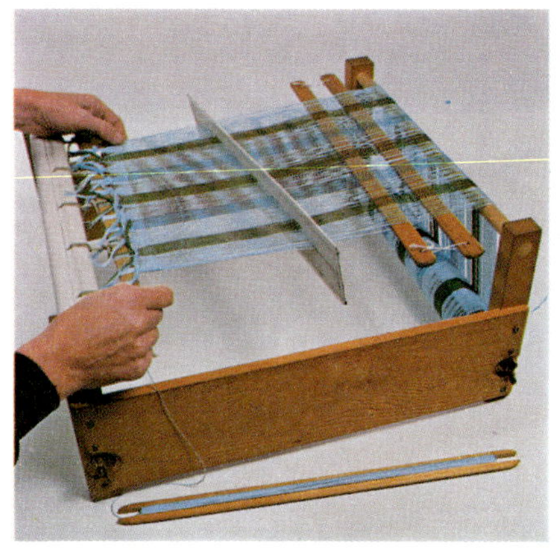

17 Control the weft at the edge of the fabric with your fingers as you pass the weft across the warp.

18 Push the weft down holding the heddle on each side. Make sure the weft is at right angles to the warp.

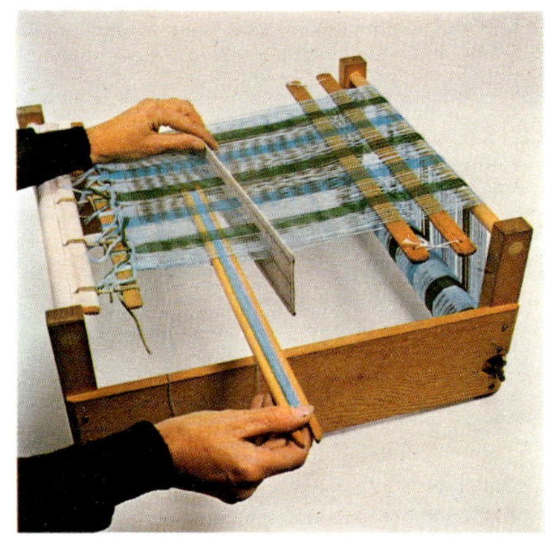

19 Push the rigid heddle down and pass the shuttle through the space between the threads.

20 Change the weft colour by taking the weft round the selvedge and into the last weft shed.

21 Weave two weft threads of the new colour and take the loose end into the second shed.

22 Wind the fabric forward on to the fabric roller frequently as your weaving progresses.

ate the warp threads at the cross and put the second lease stick through the space at the back of the heddle (13). Tie the lease sticks together at each end. Check that they are correctly in place through alternate warp threads and remove the tie from the cross at the front of the heddle. Untie the end of the warp from the front bar of the loom. Cut the warp threads across the loop at the end of the warp.

With the threading hook, select the warp threads which are over the nearest lease stick and thread them through the holes in the heddle (14). Remember to leave two double threads on each side of the warp for selvedge. Slacken the wing nuts on the clamp holding the heddle.

Work from the outside edges of the warp toward the centre. Take a group of warp threads round the stick attached to the cloth roller at the front of the loom, divide them and tie half a square knot (15). Remove the board and heddle clamp from across the loom.

Now work from the centre of the warp towards the edges. Pull the ends of the warp to tighten the half knot and tie a bow or half bow. The last bows you tie are usually tighter than the first and it is better to have the threads under more tension on the edge than in the centre of the warp. Push the lease sticks through the warp to the back of the loom. Wind the cotton weft on the stick shuttle. Lift the rigid heddle up and pass the weft yarn through the space between the warp threads (16). Control the edge of the fabric with your fingers. Make sure the weft is not pulled too tight by making an arc shape with the thread across the warp to allow for some take up as you push the weft down with the heddle (17, 18). Press the rigid heddle down to weave the next thread, and continue to weave (19). To wind the fabric forward, slacken the warp roller, turn the front roller until the fabric is about 100 mm (4 in) beyond the front bar of the top of the loom. Tighten the warp by turning the back roller. Push the lease sticks to the back of the loom. Roll the fabric forward often to prevent unevenness.

Insert one layer of warp sticks round the roller under the fabric to cover the lumps made by the ties at the end of the warp.

To join the same colour in the weft, overlap the ends across a few warp threads.

A rigid heddle loom may appear to limit you to a plain weave, but with a pick up stick it is possible to make some variations.

Thread a pick up or lease stick under alternate warp threads threaded through the slots at the back of the heddle (23). By turning the stick on edge you can weave a thick weft thread over three warp threads and under one. You will find that the thick thread will cover one of the plain weave cotton threads. Always weave at least two plain cotton wefts between the thick threads.

You can weave thick or different coloured weft threads anywhere you like in your design, they do not have to cross the width of the warp. Finish the ends of these threads by taking them round two warp threads and back into the same space. You can create interesting designs and textures with this technique, called inlaid weft.

Cut the woven fabric off the loom and divide to make table mats. Oversew the loose edges leaving a fringe.

23 Place a lease stick under alternate warp threads threaded through the slots of the heddle.

CUSHION COVERS

You will need:
Rigid heddle, threading hook
Two lease and some flat sticks
Length of webbing, and two
metal rings
Warping equipment
Dye and raffia
507 m (555 yds) or 100 g (3½ oz)
thick white worsted

This project demonstrates how to
weave, using a rigid heddle, without a loom.

Use a heddle which has eight
holes and slits per 25 mm (1 in).
The warp is 280 mm (11 in) wide
and 2.5 m (2¾ yds) long, which
allows 0.5 m (½ yd) for waste.
Fabric 250 mm (10 in) wide and 2
m (2¼ yds) is needed for the front
of two cushions, 460 × 460 mm
(18 × 18 in). Repeat this for the
back. Make the warp in white
worsted (1–6).

Tie the warp with raffia and dye
it with acid dye (see Chemical
Dyes page 61–63). By tie-dyeing
the warp you can make different
patterns in a single length of warp.

Decide which end of the warp
to start weaving (24). Place two
lease sticks through the cross in
the warp threads (7). Tie the lease
sticks together and cut the threads
at the end of the warp. Fix the
heddle in a wooden clamp. Select
each warp thread in order from
the lease sticks. Thread one warp
through each hole and two
through each slot in the heddle
(25). There will be twelve threads
to 25 mm (1 in). Tie the ends of
the warp together in bunches to
prevent them from slipping out of
the heddle. Remove the lease
sticks. Spread out the warp.

Place the two lease sticks
through the cross in the other end
of the warp. Thread a strong stick
through the loop at the end of the
warp, undo the tie round the loop

24 The two ends of the tie-dyed
warp, after the raffia bindings have
been removed.

and spread the warp threads
along the stick (26). Pull sections
of the warp forward and tie the
ends in varied lengths, with an
overhand knot, to break the
straight lines of colour made
across the warp by tie-dyeing
(26).

Tie the stick at the end of the
warp with a strong cord to a post,
tree, door knob, or anything else
suitable. Make sure the end of the
warp is not able to slip off the
stick. Remove the lease sticks.
Take sections of thread in front of
the heddle and pull them gently
until the threads are of even
tension throughout the warp.
Now you will see the pattern
made by knotting the warp to
distort the tie-dyeing.

Place the webbing, with the
metal rings at each end, across
your back. Slip a strong flat stick
400 mm (15 in) long through the
rings on each side of your waist
(27). Tie the ends of the warp to
the stick (15). Wind the plain
coloured worsted weft yarn into a
butterfly. By leaning slightly back
you can control the tension of the
warp while weaving (27). Weave
as previously described (16–19).

Wind the fabric forward, anti-
clockwise, into a tight neat roll.

25 Thread two ends of the warp
through a slot in the heddle and one
thread through a hole.

Place a flat stick about 300 mm
(12 in) long, across the top of the
fabric and tie it tightly to the waist
stick to hold the roll and prevent it
from unwinding. Slip the original
waist stick through the rings of the
strap round your waist and continue to weave.

To make the covers, sew two
460 mm (18 in) lengths together
for the front and repeat for the
back. Sew side seams with zip
opening.

For easy weaving restrict the
width of the warp to not more
than 375 mm (15 in).

For variety you can dye the
warp in different colours and
mixtures of colours. Then dip-dye
or tie-dye the weft with one of the
same colours that you have used
for the warp.

There are many colours and
colouring techniques to choose
from, but keep in mind that too
many colours and techniques
used in one design can cause con-
fusion and destroy your original
idea.

26 Pull sections of warp to distort dye pattern, and tie with an overhand knot behind warp stick.

27 Entire warp held under tension between a peg in the ground and strap round back of weaver's waist.

28 Detail of fabric showing the distortion of the tie-dyeing and surface texture of the plain weave.

Four Shaft Table Loom

A four shaft loom will weave plain and patterned fabrics, and a considerable length of fabric may be produced.

Shafts: there are four shafts suspended across the loom. Each shaft carries a number of heddles, which are held between the top and bottom bars of the shaft. Each heddle has an eyelet in the centre through which a warp thread is threaded. Each shaft can be lifted independently by pressing a lever on the loom (1). This will raise the warp threads through the eyes of the heddle on that shaft.

Reed: the reed controls the number of warp threads to 25 mm (1 in). Reeds are made with a number of wires spaced at set intervals. The spaces between the wires are known as dents. A range of sizes can be purchased. One reed should be supplied with the loom. The reed is held in position by a beater, or sley, at the front of the loom. This swings backward and forward to beat the weft yarn into the warp (1).

Rollers: the back warp roller and the front cloth roller turn and are

1 Four shaft loom with levers on the side and a reed fixed in the sley across the front of the loom.

2 Wool and worsted thread wrapped round pieces of card. Lower right design chosen for tunic.

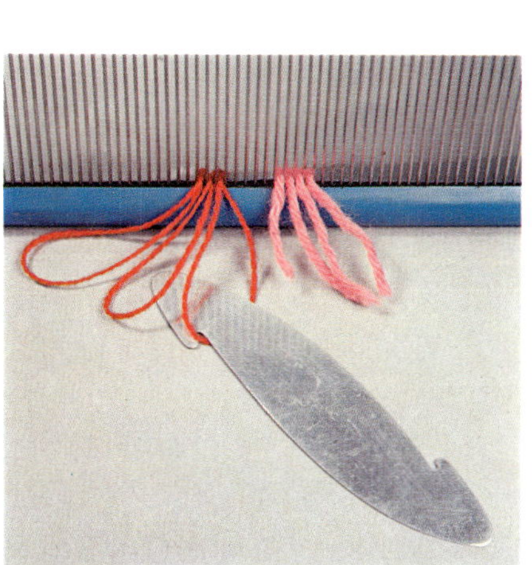

3 Reed showing slightly more space occupied by the threads than there is space left between the threads.

4 Wind the first warp thread 3 m (3½ yds) long from side to side of the warping board.

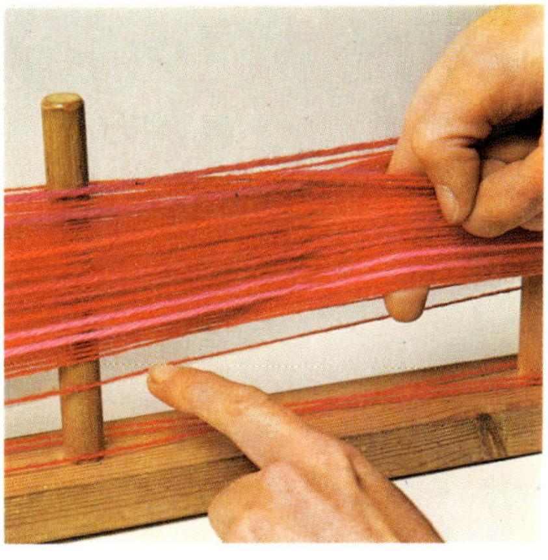

5 Wind the second warp thread in the same way as the first, completing the figure of eight at each end.

6 Join the pink worsted to the red wool by knotting them together as near to the end peg as possible.

7 Index finger between the threads at the cross and counted threads held down by the other index finger.

locked in position by a rachet wheel and pawl. Sticks for holding the warp threads are attached to these rollers.

Accessories: a pair of lease sticks will be provided with the loom. You will need to purchase or make a raddle (11) the correct length for the loom. To make a raddle, hammer 40 mm (1½ in) nails 10 mm (⅜ in) apart along a length of wood 25 × 50 mm (2 × 1 in). Stagger the nails to prevent the wood from splitting (11). You will also need stick shuttles and a warping board. Make a yarn spool holder with long nails or wooden dowels in a wooden board. Use jam jars, tins or plastic containers for holding balls of wool. If you purchase roller shuttles you will have to buy a bobbin winder (22).

TUNIC

You will need:
1700 m (1880 yds) or 450 g (15 oz) two ply wool
210 m (230 yds) or 200 g (6½ oz) four ply worsted
Warping equipment
Four shaft loom and accessories
Commercial paper pattern
Lining material

Making the warp
Wrap lengths of wool and thick worsted threads round a piece of card to give you an idea of the appearance of the warp. Make a variety of stripes of different colours and proportions (2).

Select a reed with an approximately suitable number of dents per 25 mm (1 in) for the thread used in your card design. Thread some short lengths of these yarns through the dents of the reed to check visually that you have the correct number of threads per 25 mm (1 in) (3). Using a reed with eight dents per 25 mm (1 in) there are two red wool threads in a dent for the red stripes, and two red wool and one worsted thread in a dent for coloured stripes. Now you have established that you need sixteen wool threads per 25 mm (1 in) across the whole warp and eight extra worsted threads in 25 mm (1 in).

Measure the stripes in your design (2). The red stripe for the tunic measures 19 mm (¾ in) and will need 12 wool threads. The other stripes measure 12 mm (½ in) and will need 8 wool and 4 worsted threads (2).

The warp is 3 m (3¾ yds) long, 920 mm (1 yd) for each side of the tunic, 610 mm (24 in) for waste and 530 mm (21 in) of extra warp for samples. The width of the warp is 530 mm (21 in) with a total of 424 threads. You will need 1300 m (1422 yds) of two ply wool for 356 warp threads, including 4 extra warp threads for selvedge, and 400 m (438 yds) for weft woven at about 10 threads to 25 mm (1 in). You will need 210 m (230 yds) of thick worsted for 68 warp threads.

Make the warp in the following order, using your own colours, and including 2 extra warp threads each side for selvedge:
14 red wool
Repeat the following four times:
1 pink worsted, 2 wool, × 4
12 wool
1 purple worsted, 2 wool, × 4
12 wool
1 tangerine worsted, 2 wool, × 4
12 wool
1 cerise worsted, 2 wool, × 4
12 wool
End the warp with:
1 pink worsted, 2 wool, × 4
14 wool

The warping board (4) may have pegs fixed in it, if not, you will need to place pegs the correct distance apart. Pegs are needed on each side of the board for every metre (39 in) of the warp. There should be three pegs at the beginning and at the end of the warp for making the cross. Place the spools or balls of yarn and some scissors to hand near the warping board.

Tie the first wool thread loosely to the peg at the top left hand corner of the warping board. Take this thread over the second peg, under the third peg, round the peg at the top right hand corner, round the peg on the left, over the fourth and third peg from the bottom on the right, under the second peg to the first peg on the right. You have made one warp thread (4).

Now take this thread over the second peg on the right, under the third peg, over the fourth peg, round the peg on the left, round the peg in the top right hand corner, over the third peg, under the second peg to the first peg. This is your second warp thread (5).

Check that you have made a figure of eight cross with these two threads at each end of the warp (5). Refer back to the details for making the warp and you will see that you need to make 14 wool threads before changing the yarn.

Knot the pink worsted thread to the red wool with the knot as near as possible to the first peg. Wind one warp thread. Knot the red wool to the worsted and wind two warp threads, then repeat this 4 times (6). Continue to make the warp referring back for the details. To count the threads, insert your index finger between the threads at the cross, pull the index finger forward against the threads, this will release the first warp thread, and so on (7). This type of thread is rather bulky and the threads soon reach the top of

the pegs on the warping board, so make the warp in two halves. Tie the warp tightly, with a strong thread, round the loop at each end by the peg. Tie a thread through the cross, down by one peg and up by the other, at each end of the warp (8). Tie the threads together at intervals along the length of the warp (8). It is important to check that you have tied the warp correctly. Slide the warp off the pegs at the bottom of the warping board, and wind it into a ball, tucking the end under the outside layer of threads (9, 10).

8 Secure both crosses with a tie. Tie tightly through loop at each end and at intervals round warp.

10 The completed warp with the end for raddling coming from the centre of the ball.

Setting the warp on the loom

Tie the raddle firmly on to each end of the warp bar at the back of the loom (11).

Place the balls of warp on the table in front of the loom. Take the end of the warp coming from the centre of each ball and find the loop at each end where the warp has been tied (10).

Slide the two warps on to the stick in the correct position and the right way round for the design. The knots in the cross tie should be on the same side of each warp (11). Remove the tie round the loop at the end of each warp

9 Grasp warp with end hanging down to your elbow, wind the threads firmly round your hand.

11 Slide loop at the end of each warp on to the stick attached to warp roller at the back of loom.

(12). Pull the tie on each side of the cross to separate the warp.

Insert two lease sticks and tie them together at each end, leaving about 25 mm (1 in) between the sticks (13). Check that the lease sticks are correctly placed in the warp and remove the tie from the cross. Measure the raddle to make sure the warp threads will be in the centre of the loom.

Hold the warp threads under tension above the nails in the raddle and you will see them crossing in a figure of eight between the lease sticks (13).

There are 16 wool threads to 25 mm (1 in) and the worsted threads are extra warp threads at 8 to 25 mm (1 in). Select the threads from the lease making sure they are not twisted between the lease and the raddle. Place groups of warp threads in each 10 mm (½ in) space between the nails in the raddle (13) in the following order:

7 red wool

7 red wool

6 red wool, 4 worsted

Repeat until you have completed the raddling with 7 red wool in the last group to include the selvedge. Take care not to lift the warp so that the threads come out of the raddle. If the raddle has a top, place this in position. Remove the lease sticks.

Spread the threads at the end of the warp evenly along the warp stick. Tie the cords which have been undone between this stick and the warp roller. Move the heddles to the side of each harness. Give the warp a few firm tugs to even out the tension of the threads before removing the ties. Keep the warp under tension and wind the threads once round the warp roller.

At this stage wind in a layer of warp sticks placed 50 mm (2 in) apart to give an even surface to the warp. Give the warp a few more tugs and wind it round the roller several times until the edge of the warp has built up and is likely to slip (14). Repeat this until there are about 600 mm (24 in) of warp left unwound.

Remove the raddle from the loom. Pull the string tie on each side of the lease and place the lease sticks through the cross at the end of the warp. Tie the lease sticks together leaving a space of 100 mm (4 in) between them to enable you to move them easily along the warp (15). Check that the lease sticks are correctly positioned in the warp and remove the cross tie. Remove the reed and the top of the reed holder or sley (15). To move the lease sticks back through the warp before threading, pull a section of threads at a time, below the front lease stick down and then above this lease stick up. When the warp threads are even, cut across the loop at the end of the warp removing the knots made when warping. Divide the warp into sections, and secure each section with a slip knot.

12 Insert one lease stick through each space on either side of the cross in the warp.

13 Count the threads at the cross between lease sticks, place each group in spaces between raddle nails.

14 Place another layer of warp sticks in the spaces between last layer to even the surface of warp.

15 Rest the lease sticks across the two long sticks placed through the loom on each side.

Threading the loom

You will need 176 heddles on shafts one and two, and 34 heddles on shafts three and four. Count the heddles from the centre of each shaft, half on each side. Thread from either side unless the heddles can be removed from one side only of the shaft, in which case start threading the loom from the other side.

Take a loop of strong thread round the ends of the first section of the warp and tie it to the cloth bar or cloth roller of the loom to keep the warp under tension. The same loop of thread can be used for the next sections (19).

Select the warp threads in the correct order from the lease sticks (16). Pull each warp thread with a threading hook or fingers through the eye of a heddle on the harnesses (17). Thread in the following order:

the first wool thread on shaft one, the second on shaft two. Repeat five times more. Thread the first two threads double for selvedge. Thread the first worsted on shaft three. Thread wool on shaft one and shaft two followed by the second worsted on shaft four. Repeat once again.

When you have threaded a section of the pattern, check that the threads are in the correct order and on the right shafts. Tie each section with a slip knot (18). When the threading is complete, release the warp roller and pull the warp forward through the heddles about 250 mm (9 in). Place the reed in the sley and replace the top.

On a 610 mm (24 in) loom start threading the reed 25 mm (1 in) in from the end. Select the warp threads in the same order as they were entered in the heddles with the fingers of one hand.

Draw the threads through the dents of the reed with a reed hook

16 Select each warp thread in the order of one over and one under the nearest lease stick.

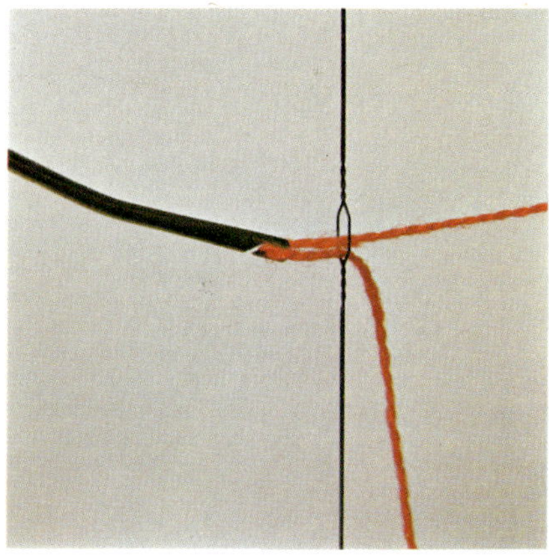

17 Draw each warp thread through the eye of the heddle with the threading hook facing downwards.

18 Check that the threads are in correct order on right shafts and tie each group with a slip knot.

19 Thread two red wool warp threads through each dent of the reed with a reed hook.

20 Thread the worsted thread, which is an extra thread, with two wool threads through a dent of the reed.

21 Divide and tie each group of threads round the stick attached to the cloth roller.

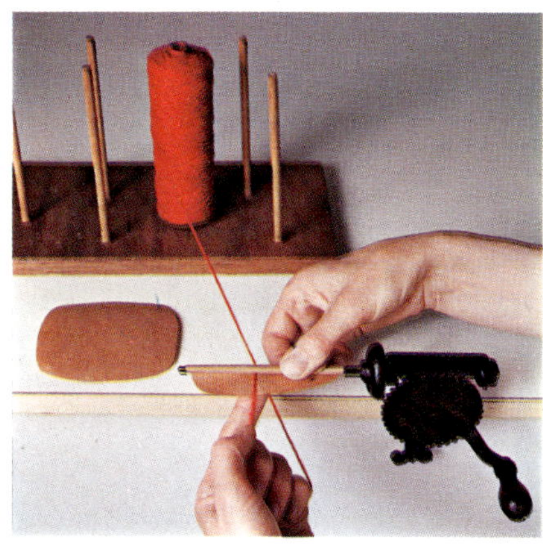

22 Wind paper firmly round the spindle catching in the end of the red wool.

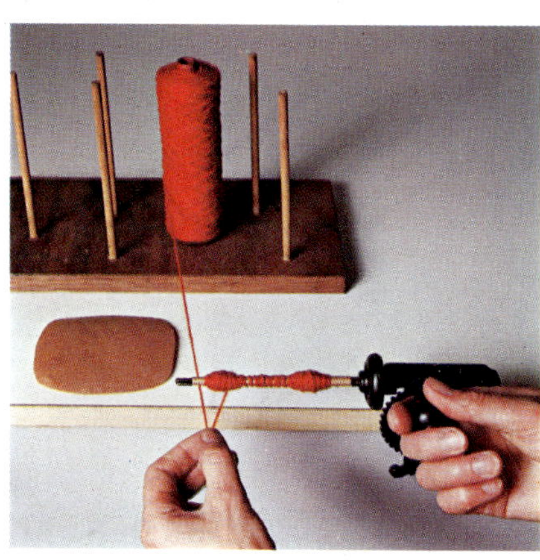

23 Turn the handle of the bobbin winder and make a bump of yarn at each end of the paper.

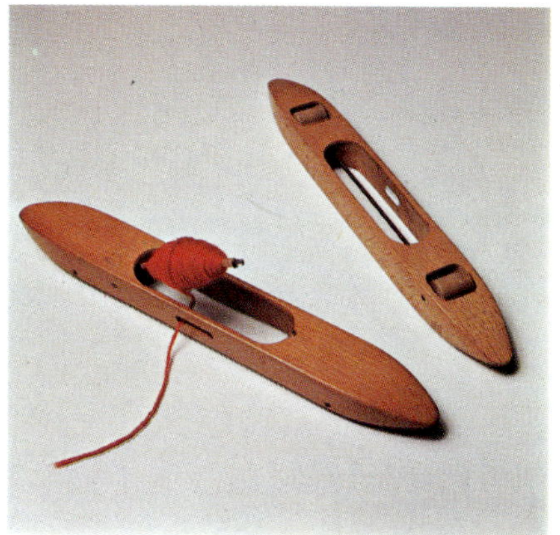

24 Release the spindle and insert the bobbin into the shuttle with the red wool through the slot.

in the other hand (19, 20). Take sections of warp threads not more than 25 mm (1 in) wide and pull them to even out the tension.

Work from the outside edges of the warp and tie them with half a square knot (21). Working from the centre of the warp towards the edges, pull the ends of the warp to tighten the knots and tie a bow. Push the lease sticks to the back of the loom and remember to keep them well back while you are weaving. Wind the red wool yarn on to a stick shuttle.

To weave with a roller shuttle, you will need to buy a bobbin winder. Cut some rectangles of wrapping paper and round off the corners (22). Wind the yarn backwards and forwards on to the bobbin, always keeping a bump of yarn at each end and never taking the yarn over the highest point of the bump (23). Fix the bobbin into the roller shuttle (24).

WEAVING A TUNIC

When weaving with a roller shuttle the slot of the shuttle should face towards you with the rollers on the lower warp shed (25).

Grip the shuttle between thumb and fingers with the palm of the hand facing up (25). Throw the shuttle through the shed of the warp with the other hand against the reed in the same position to catch it (26).

To start weaving, press the first lever on the loom to raise the threads on shaft one (26). Pass the weft through the shed of the warp with the shuttle as near to the reed as possible since this is the widest space between the threads.

Leave the weft in an arc shape across the warp and control the

25 Press second lever to raise red warp on shaft two leaving the extra warp on the back of the fabric.

26 Press the first lever to raise red warp on shaft one leaving extra warp on the back of the fabric.

27 Press second, third and fourth levers to raise half red warp and extra warp to face of fabric.

28 Press first, third and fourth levers to raise half red warp and extra warp to face of fabric.

edge of the fabric with your fingers. Hold the sley in the centre and beat the weft down once or twice but not more to weave quickly and evenly.

Release the first lever. Press the second lever to raise shaft two and insert the next weft thread (25). Continue to weave alternately on these two shafts until the warp is evenly spaced across the loom. Check the weaving for any errors in the threading of the warp.

To start weaving the pattern press the first, third and fourth levers, one at a time, to raise three shafts for the first weft thread (28). Press the second, third and fourth levers to raise three shafts for the second weft (27). Repeat the first and second wefts. Repeat the first weft again. End the repeat of the pattern by pressing the second lever.

You have now woven six weft threads and completed one repeat of the pattern. Continue weaving this design (see draft page 48).

Slacken the cloth roller and check that you are weaving about 10 weft threads to 25 mm (1 in).

To move the fabric forward on the loom, make sure the shafts are down, release the warp roller, turn the cloth roller and insert some sticks between the fabric and the roller to cover any bumps made by knots. When the edge of the fabric is about 100 mm (4 in) from the cloth bar, tension the warp by turning the warp roller.

Study the section on drafting, read the order of lifting from the bottom to the top and you will see that you have woven the section using shafts one and two for spacing the warp. You have also woven the first repeats for the hem of the front of the tunic. To continue the design for the tunic refer to the drafts (page 48 and 49).

Repeat the first section ten times and the second section twice, as indicated by the arrows in the draft, and continue to weave the pattern repeating the last section six times.

To weave the back of the tunic repeat the first section of the draft twenty-five times.

Use a commercial paper pattern to cut out and make up your length of woven fabric. Line throughout to finish.

Pattern drafting
Such a variety of patterns can be made on this loom that it is important to understand the basic principles of drafting.

Threading draft: the spaces between the horizontal lines represent the four shafts. The shaft nearest the weaver at the front of the loom is number one and the shaft at the back of the loom is number four. The mark in the space between the horizontal lines indicates the heddle on the shaft through which the warp should be threaded. A heavier mark in the threading draft indicates a thick thread.

Lifting plan: the noughts in the

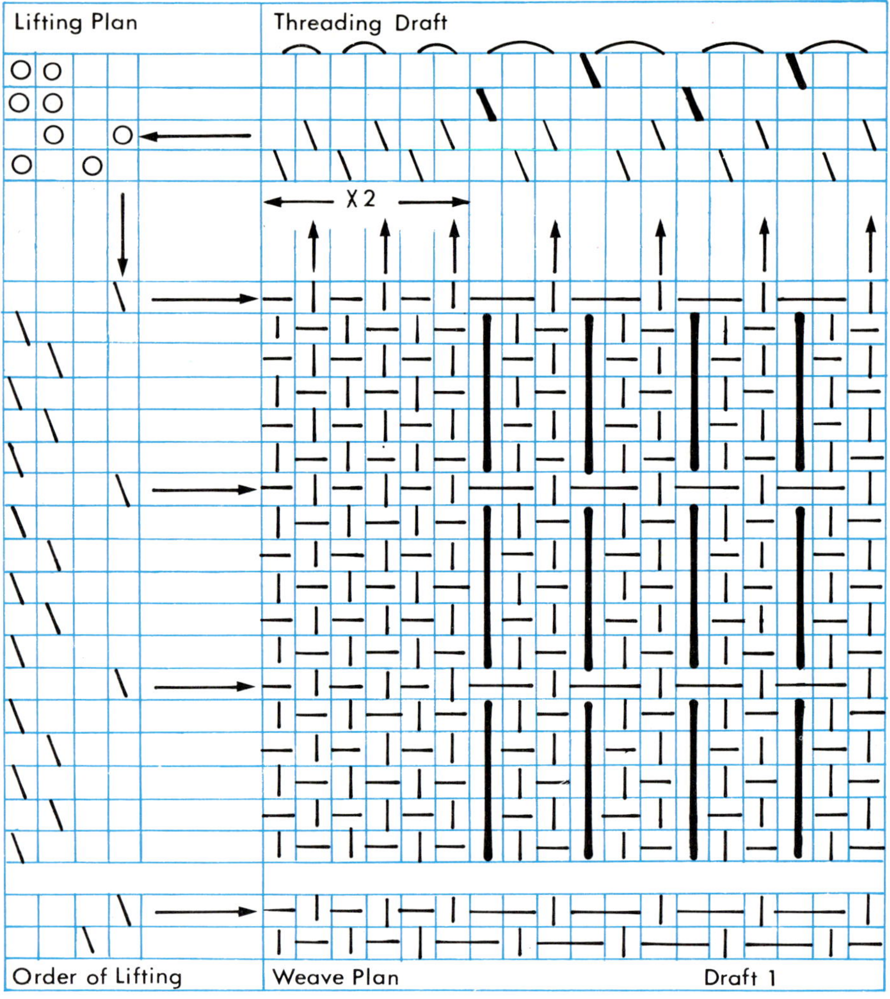

Threading draft showing pattern for hem and first (lower) section of tunic.

squares between the horizontal lines indicate which shafts should be raised for weaving. On a table loom the levers are pressed down to raise the shafts.

Order of lifting: the marks in the squares between the vertical lines give the order in which the levers should be pressed down for each weft thread in the pattern. A heavier mark in the square indicates that a thick weft thread should be used.

Weave plan: this is a plan of the weave on the face of the fabric.

The warp threads are shown as vertical lines in the squares of the graph paper.

It is important to understand that when a shaft is lifted, all the threads on that shaft are raised. Study the weave plan and you will see where all the threads on shaft two are raised to the face of the fabric. The arrow pointing up from the weave plan shows that these threads are threaded through the heddles on shaft two. The arrow pointing to the left to the lifting plan shows which lever to press to raise shaft two. The arrow pointing down to the order

of lifting indicates when to raise shaft two. The arrow pointing right shows the threads on shaft two raised to the face of the fabric in the weave plan.

Use this method of drafting as a formula for understanding patterns shown in other books.

Samples or other options
You have now discovered that the basic fabric is made of red wool woven in plain weave and the pattern is made by either raising the extra warp threads to the surface of the fabric or by keeping them down to the back of the fabric. Block designs and blocks combined with stripes can be made this way (29, 30). When weaving on a four shaft loom, the threads are controlled by the levers to make patterns which repeat across the loom. You can also manipulate threads with your fingers to make an entirely original design.

To make a leno twist, miss a section of extra warp threads with the shuttle by changing the levers in the middle of inserting a weft thread, as indicated by the two lifts in the order of lifting (see draft for 31). This makes a section of extra warp threads on the surface of the fabric. Half way through weaving this section, cross the worsted threads with your fingers taking the weft up through the warp in the centre of the stripe, round the two crossing threads and back into the same place between the warp threads (see the cross in the lifting plan in draft for 31).

Inlaid weft is an extra weft used entirely to decorate the surface of a fabric. This weft is woven under the extra warp at any place across the width of the fabric (32, 33, 34).

The warp can be cut to make fringes in the fabric. Cut the extra

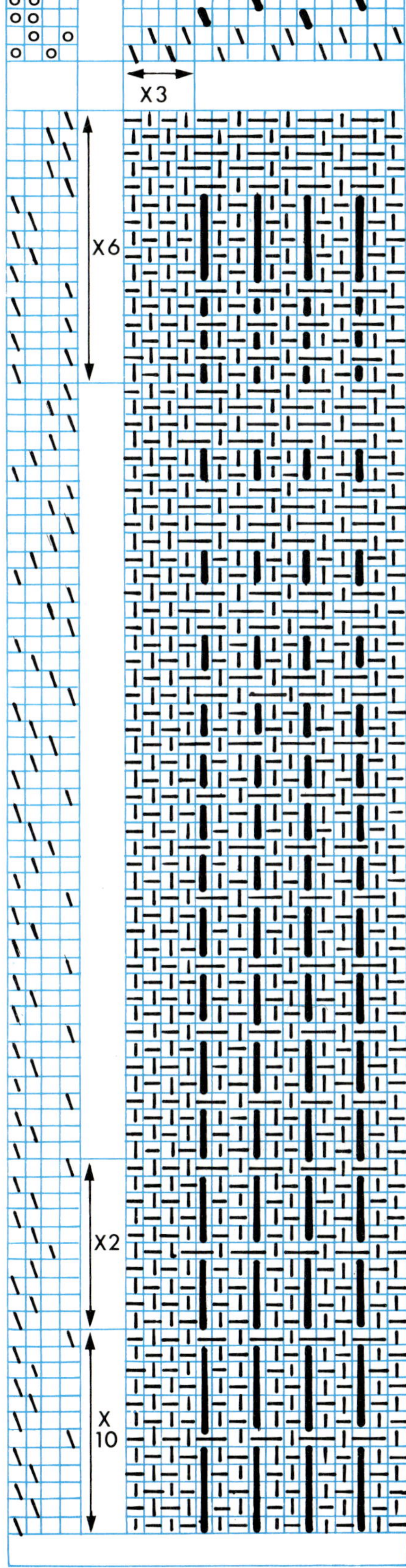

X3
X6
X2
X
10

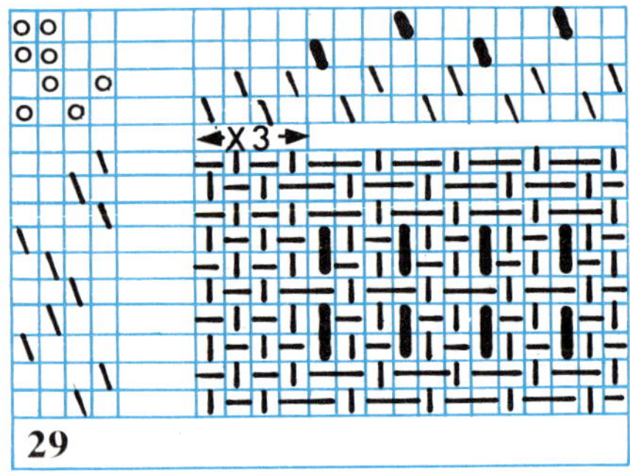

29

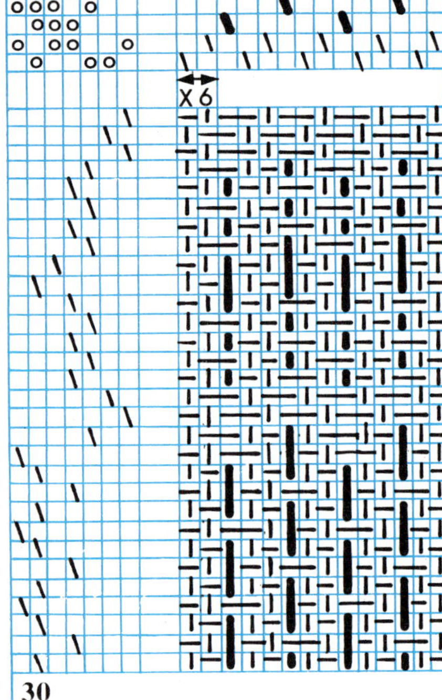

30

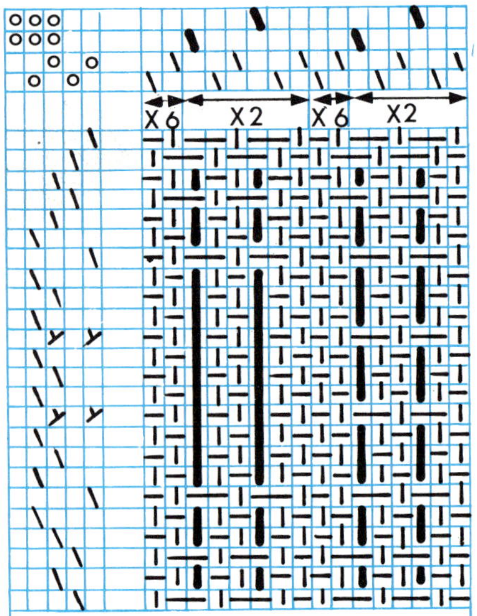

31

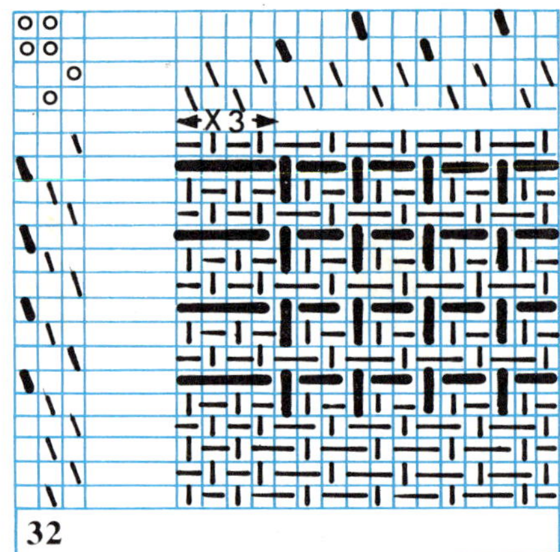

32

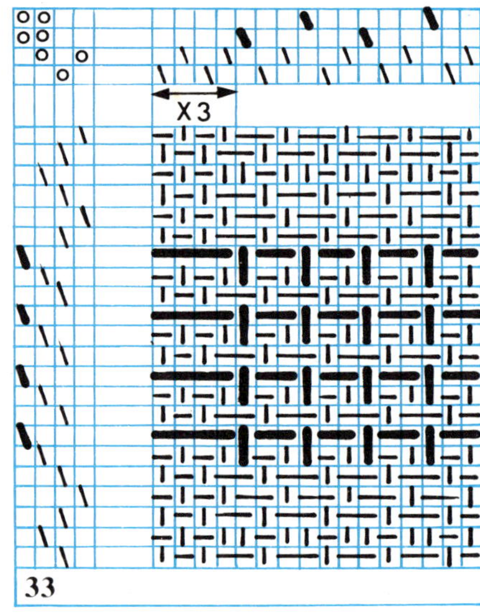

33

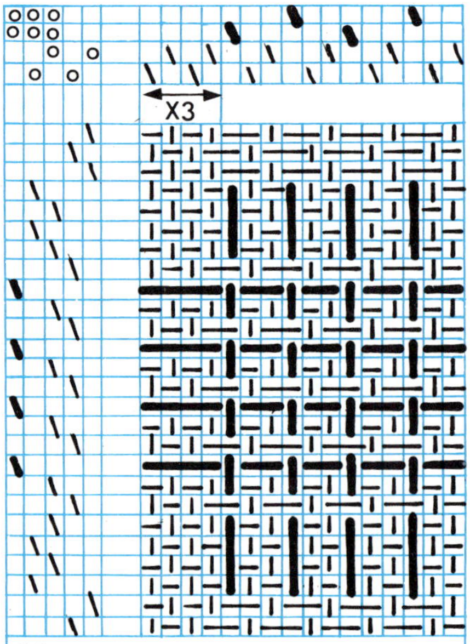

34

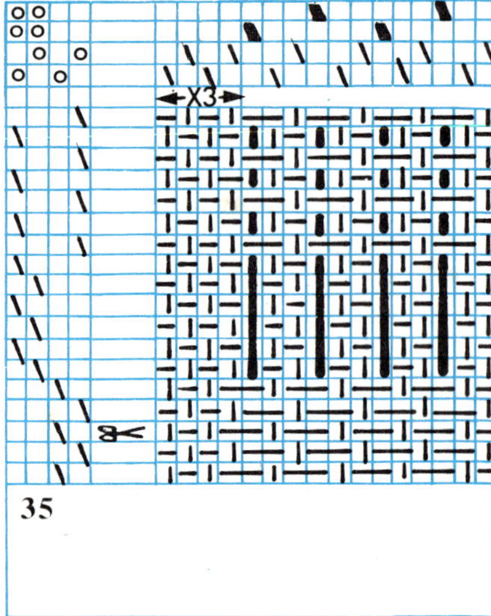

35

warp threads on the back of the fabric to prevent a mark being made on the front by loose fibres. Cut where shown in the draft (35).

Extra warp gives freedom for variety in the use of colour and proportion from one side of the fabric to the other. It is easy to manipulate the shafts to give a wide range of designs, used singly or put together, to make many exciting fabrics for dress or furnishing.

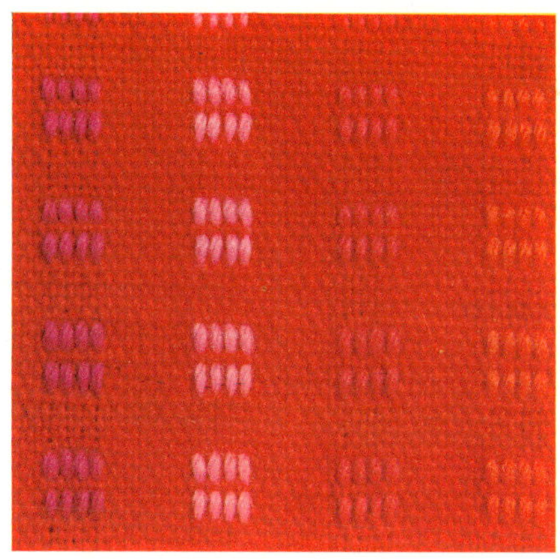

29 Block design made by floating extra warp threads over two wefts, under one, over two and under five.

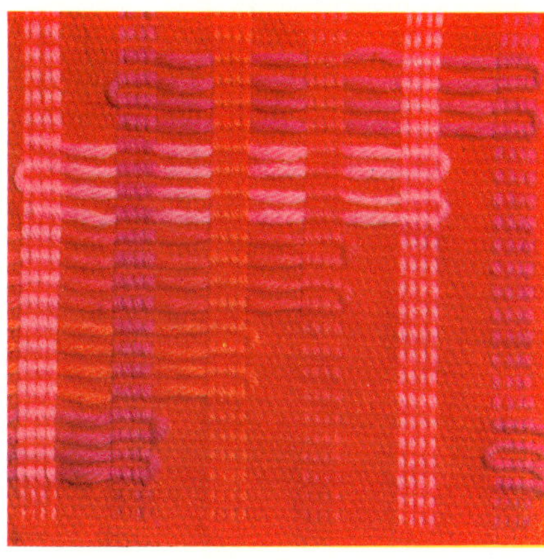

32 Inlaid worsted weft woven under the extra warp threads between every two wefts of red wool.

35 Extra warp cut at the back of fabric, as indicated in threading draft, with one cut row pulled out.

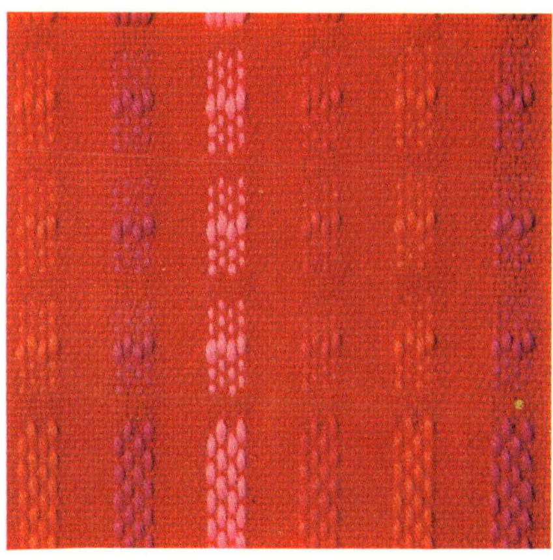

30 Extra warp raised alternately over one weft and under next with longer warp floats of three.

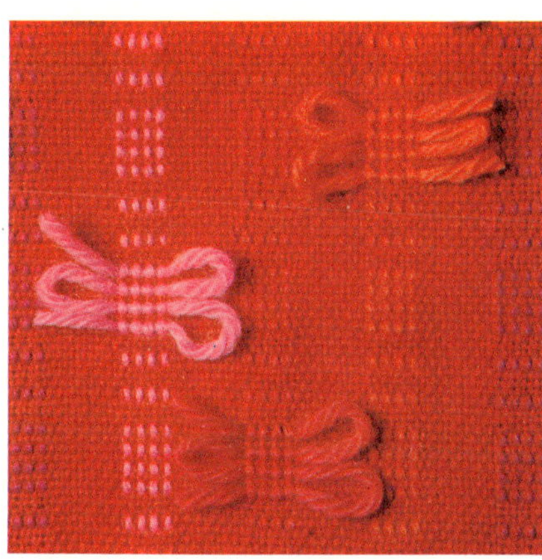

33 Inlaid worsted weft woven under the extra warp stripes leaving loops of weft at the sides.

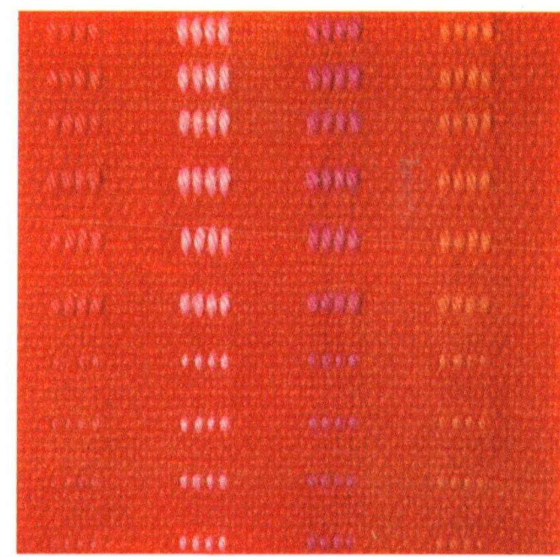

36 Extra warp threads floating over one or two, and under two to five weft threads as desired.

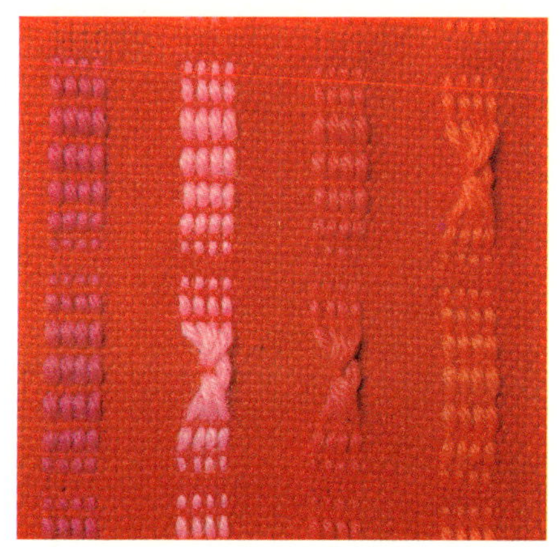

31 Leno twist in the extra warp made by crossing the threads by hand as required in the design.

34 Inlaid worsted weft woven under alternate extra warp stripes with the ends cut to make a fringe.

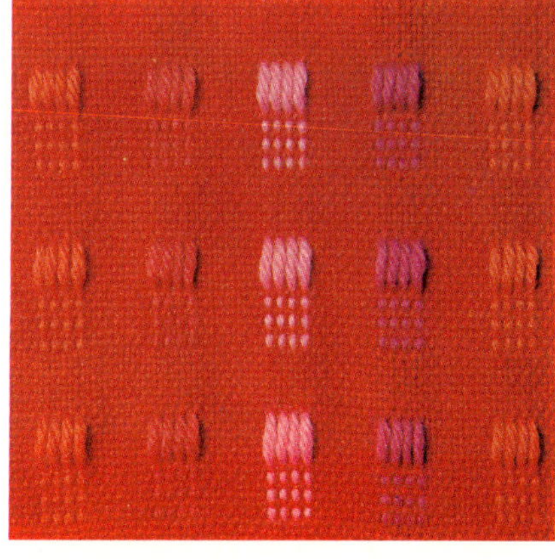

37 Block design made by floating extra warp threads over and under one three times and over six wefts.

Four Shaft Weaves

Plain weave
A simple interlacing of alternate threads. The weave can only be varied by the use of different weights and textures of yarn, and by the number of warp and weft threads to 25 mm (1 in) (1).

Hopsack weave
A plain weave with the threads interlacing in pairs. This gives a coarse appearance but a softer fabric (2).

Extra weft rib weave
A small rib effect making a firm hardwearing fabric suitable for upholstery. Try changing the colour in the extra weft (3).

Twill weave
A variety of twills can be made to produce diagonal lines across the fabric. A 2/2 twill is suitable for suiting and dress fabric (4). Reverse the direction of the twill weave for a zig-zag effect (5). To make a smooth surface use a 3/1 twill with either the warp or the weft on the face of the fabric. If you change the weave from warp to weft face, to produce horizontal stripes, reverse the direction of the weave to lock the weft against the warp on the edge of the stripe

1 A plain weave fabric with warp and weft threads interlacing alternately. (Top of draft below.)

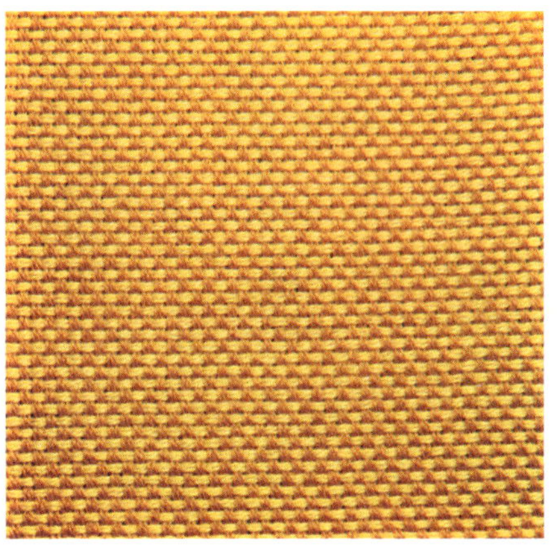

2 A hopsack weave, with two warp and weft threads weaving as one. (Middle of draft below.)

3 Extra weft weave with alternate threads in plain weave between thicker white threads. (Lower draft.)

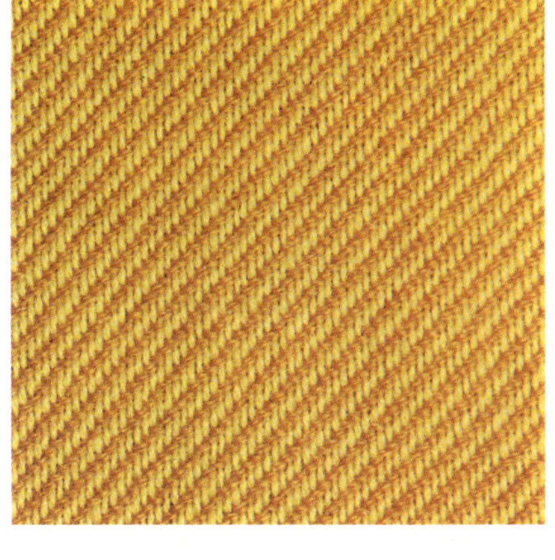

4 A 2/2 twill weave used to produce diagonal lines on the face and back of the fabric. (Top of draft left.)

5 A 2/2 reverse twill used to change direction of diagonal lines on face and back. (Bottom of draft left.)

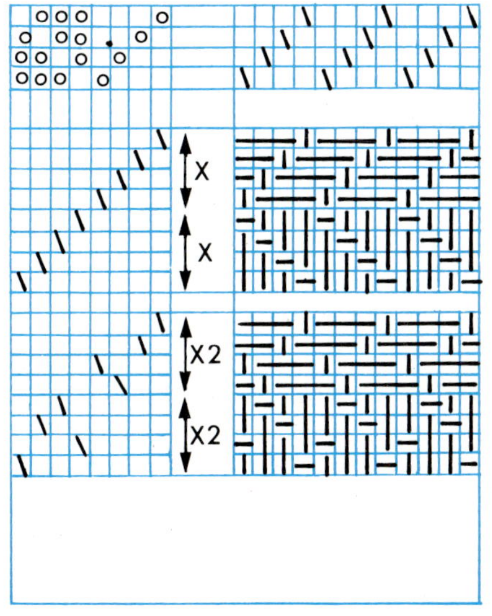

6 A 3/1 twill arranged in irregular stripes showing first weft and then warp. (Top of draft left.)

7 A satin weave with warp and a sateen weave with weft in regular stripes. (Bottom of draft left.)

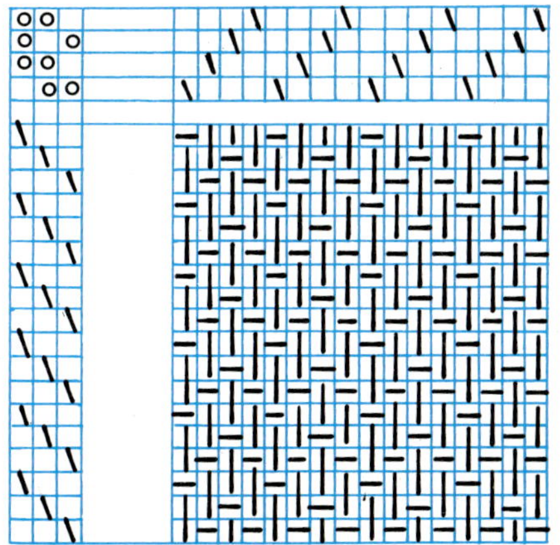

Draft for 8 and 9 above shows how weft gives appearance of plain weave on the face of the fabric.

8 Small pattern motifs on a plain coloured ground made by using brown as one of weft threads.

9 The pattern is small in width but not in length if you weave a long section before changing the colours.

and to prevent the weft threads from slipping (6).

Satin and sateen weaves

Use satin or sateen weaves for the same reasons as you would a 3/1 twill except that you are breaking the diagonal (7). To make horizontal stripes, work in multiples of four weft threads and the warp will lock automatically against the weft at the edge of the stripes (see drafts for 6, 7). These weaves are interesting woven on a coloured striped warp. The stripe is almost covered by the weft faced weave and shows strongly in the warp faced weave.

Patterned rug weave

The face of the fabric gives the appearance of plain weave but alternate weft threads float across three warp threads at the back of the fabric (drafts 8, 9, and Heading). Make a warp with thick cotton at 4 threads to 25 mm (1 in). Use two ply carpet wool, double, for weft. The patterns are produced by continuously changing the colour of the weft.

Herringbone weave

A twill reversed in direction from a central point in the threading

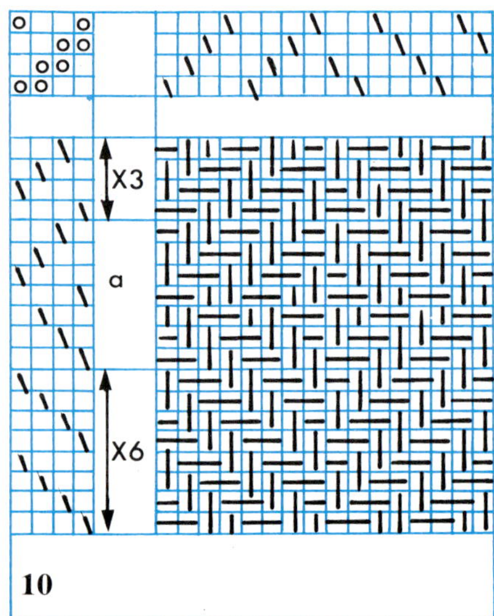

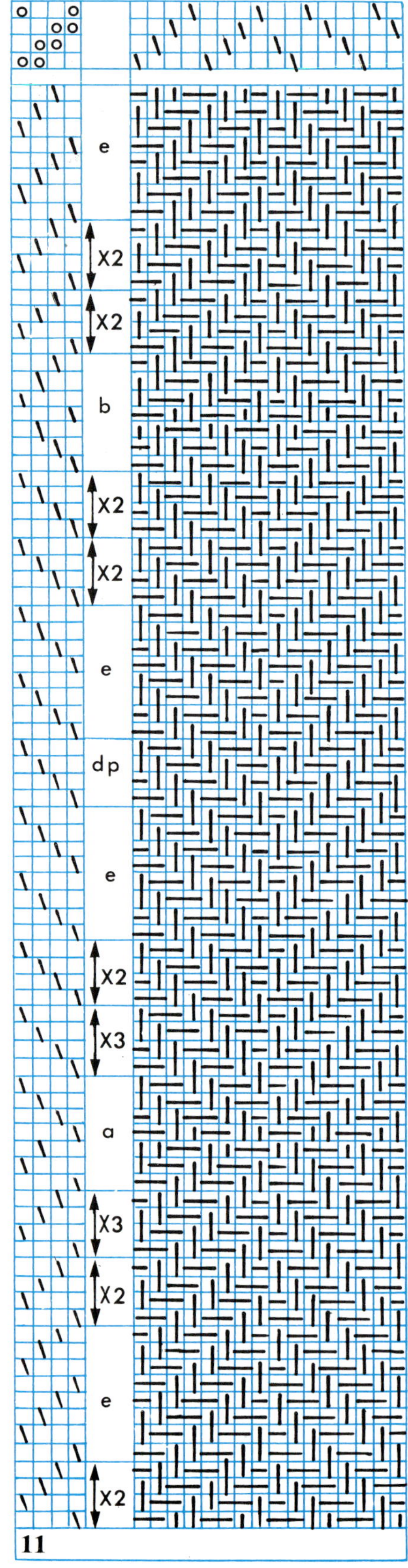

54

draft to produce a striped twill effect. This can be regular, or varied with different sized stripes. For a clearly defined pattern use contrasting tones of colour. This shows in the skirt where the lightest blue weft crosses the darkest blue warp.

HERRINGBONE SKIRT

You will need:
3184 m (3406 yds) or 950 g (2 lbs) two ply wool in shades of blue and purple
Four shaft loom and accessories
Commercial paper pattern

The skirt is made in six panels. Each panel is 508 mm (20 in) wide and 1 m (39 in) long. Make the weft in dark purple (dp), light purple (p) and five shades of blue (a-e) from light to dark. Make the warp 7 m (7⅝ yds) long, including waste, in three shades of blue, at 14 threads per 25 mm (1 in).

Weave according to the draft (10) reading upwards from the hem at the base. Repeat each section as indicated by the arrows in the following order of weft colour: 4a, 4b, 4c, 4d, 4c, 4b, 4a, × 2, 7a, 4b, 4c, 4d (draft 10). Continue according to draft 11:

4p, 4dp, 8e, 4dp, 4p, 4d, 4c, 4b, 7a, 4b, 4c, 4d, 4p, 4dp, 8e, 4dp, 8e, 4dp, 4p, 4d, 4c, 7b, 4c, 4d, 4p, 4dp, 8e.

Weave at 12 wefts to 25mm (1 in). You have finished the weave shown in the draft and now know the pattern. Continue weaving, leaving out one of the lighter blue weft colours when changing the direction of the weave. Add extra dark blue and dark purple stripes between the bands of lighter blue. When you have woven six lengths for the skirt, weave the waist bands. Following pattern cut out and make up the skirt.

1 Insert a padding thread of thick wool, using a heddle as a needle, under the weft floats on the back.

2 Bedford cord weave to make rounded cords in direction of warp with plain weave on the face of cords.

3 Distorted weft weave having three wefts in one plain weave shed on alternate warp stripes.

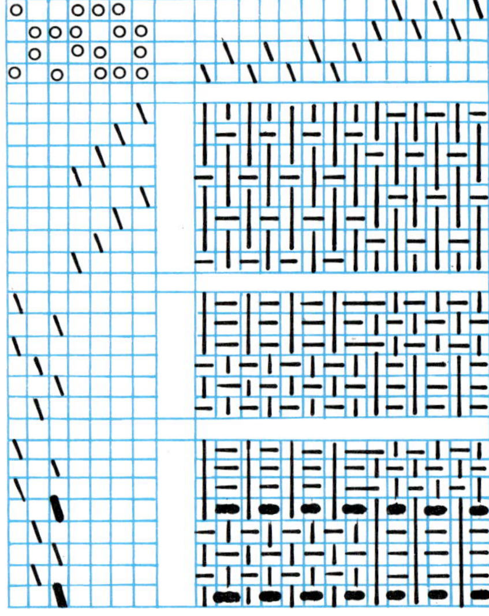

BEDFORD CORD CUSHION COVERS

You will need:
993 m (1086 yds) or 350 g (12 oz) brown wool
869 m (950 yds) or 230 g (8 oz) coloured wools
Four shaft loom and accessories

Thread the brown wool on shafts one and two. Make a warp 2.75 m (3 yds) long, 508 mm (20 in) wide with 16 threads to 25 mm (1 in). The draft shows bedford cord (top), distorted weft (centre), and another distorted

weft using thick or different colour thread for every fourth weft (lower). Weave bedford cord with alternate coloured weft threads. You can pad all, none, alternate or groups of cords (1).

Make up woven length into cushion covers as illustrated.

HONEYCOMB WEAVE BLANKET

You will need:
3568 m (3900 yds) or 4½ k (10 lb) thick bouclé wool
Four shaft loom and accessories

The blanket is 1.84 × 3 m (6 × 10 ft), and made in four panels. To weave this bulky fabric on a table loom, you will have to weave two lengths and thread the loom again for another two. Make each warp 7 m (7½ yds) long, 483 mm (19 in) wide, with 6 warp threads to 25 mm (1 in).

One dark follows five light threads in the warp. Thread the dark threads through the heddles on shaft four (see draft). Three light follow one dark thread in the weft. Weave a dark thread when you raise shaft one, and a light thread when you raise shafts two, three and four (see draft). Weave at 8 weft threads to 25 mm (1 in). Stitch the panels together with a running stitch three warp threads from the edge of the fabric. Decorate the join with cross-lacing through the dark warp threads on the front of the fabric (1). Oversew fringes at each end with blue wool.

Try weaving a honeycomb with three dark threads on shafts three and four. This makes the same design on each side of the fabric.

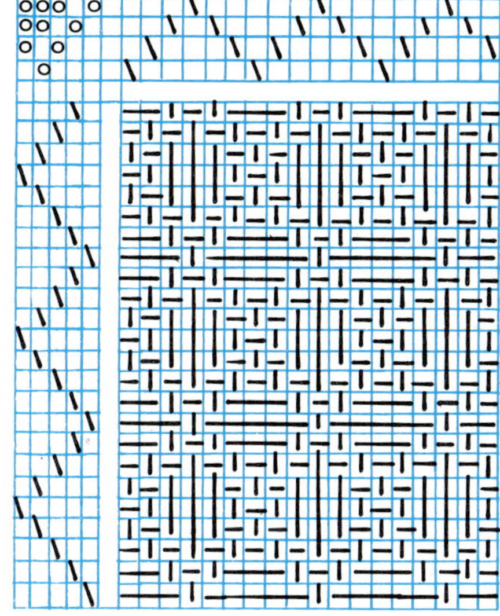

1 Honeycomb weave in which warp and weft threads form ridges and hollows on both sides of fabric.

Spinning

You can make or find for yourself everything you will need to start spinning with a spindle.

In the country you can often find sheep's wool caught in the hedges and fences, and you can sometimes buy a whole fleece after sheep shearing in the spring. Wool fibres can also be bought from suppliers of weaving and spinning equipment.

The fibres vary in colour and quality according to the individual breed of sheep. There are variations of long, coarse, short and fine fibres. Black sheep have dark grey or brown fibres (1). Before spinning, tease out your wool to remove knots, dust, dirt and thorns (2).

A spindle has two component parts, the shaft and the weight. The weights vary from about 85–100 g (3–4 oz). Spindles are sold commercially, and a supplier will advise a beginner on the best type to buy. You can make your own spindle with a length of dowel or garden cane 300–380 mm (12–15 in) long with a point at one end of the shaft. Insert the point of the shaft into half a potato, a wooden table mat or anything else you can find as a suitable weight of about 85 g

1 Samples of raw black and white fleece of different kinds as it comes from the sheep.

2 Tease out the fleece by gently separating the fibres to make a thin, even layer.

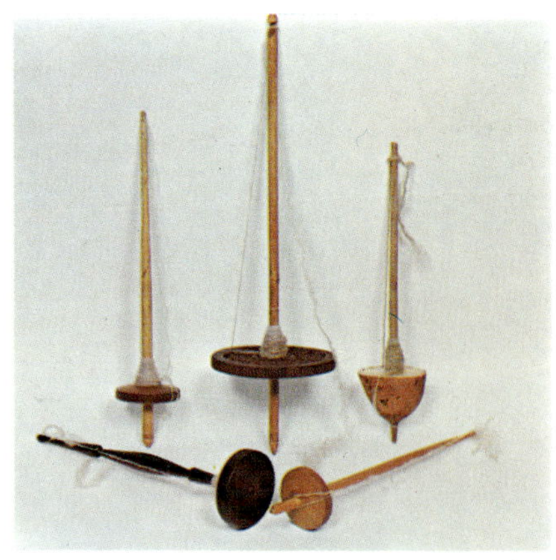

3 Spindles of various weights and sizes for you to either purchase or make for yourself.

4 Loop the thread attached to the spindle round the shaft below the spindle weight.

(3 oz) (3). About 50 mm (2 in) of the pointed end should protrude from below the spindle weight (4).

Knot a length of plied yarn, preferably wool, to the shaft of the spindle. Wind this round the shaft and fix it in position to prevent it coming undone (4, 5).

Join the teased wool to the thread by holding the thread and the fibres between the thumb and fingers of one hand while twisting the shaft of the spindle with the other hand (6, 7). This twist immediately gives strength to the join in the yarn.

As the spindle is turning, pull the fibres out from the teased wool and slide the finger and thumb upwards along the fibres as they twist into a thread and then pull down more fibres (8).

Never allow the twist in the thread to pass the finger and thumb of the hand holding the layer of fibres or they will be impossible to pull out.

Before the spindle starts to turn backwards twist the shaft again (7). When the spindle reaches the ground, wind the yarn on to the shaft (9, 4, 5) and continue to spin.

When you start to spin, you are likely to overspin the thread (10) but practice will enable you to pull the fibres out more quickly and make a good thread.

Wind the yarn from the spindle into a ball for plying or into a hank for washing. Yarn is always plied in the opposite direction from the way it was spun so as not to increase the twist. Place the balls of handspun yarn in separate containers and twist your spindle anti-clockwise.

As the spindle turns, pull the two threads from between the fingers and thumb of one hand and slide the finger and thumb of the other hand along the threads

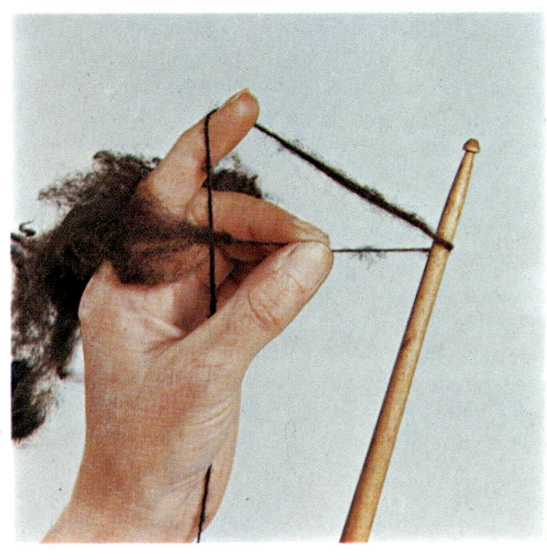

5 Take the thread to the top of the shaft and put a slip loop round the top of the spindle.

6 To join teased wool to thread separate fibres of spun thread and insert tip of wool into the V shape.

7 Twist the spindle like a top in a clockwise direction to set the spindle turning.

8 While the spindle is turning pull the fibres out between the thumb and index finger of both hands.

9 When the spindle reaches the ground stop and wind thread on to shaft and attach it to the spindle.

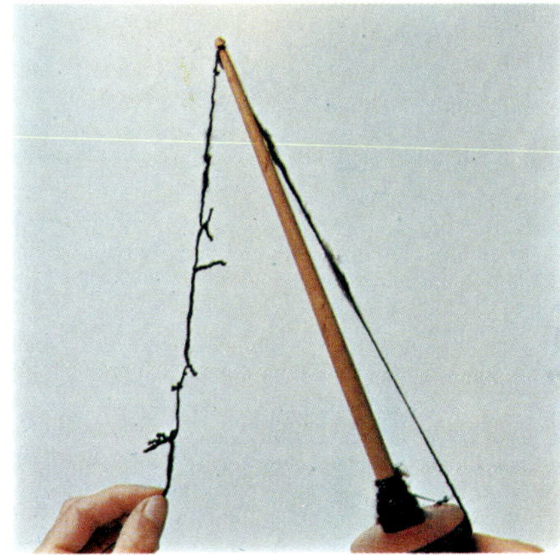

10 This is a test to see if you are over spinning the fibres. You should not have so much double twisting.

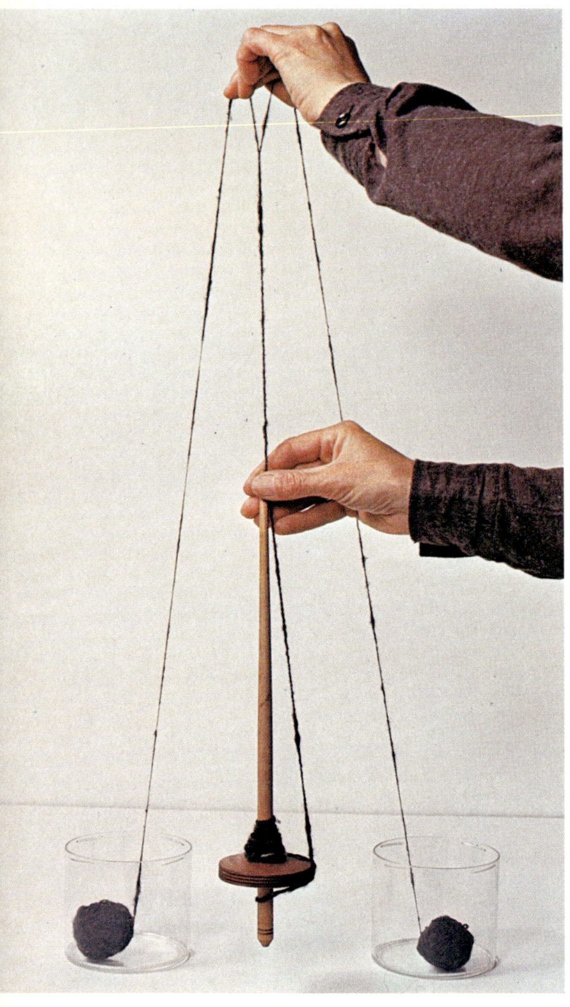

12 Wind the thread from the spindle round from thumb to elbow to make a hank in preparation for washing.

13 Hanks of handspun unwashed wool in the foreground and washed yarn displayed in the background.

14 Natural brown and white fibres spun and plied to give a textured yarn washed after plying.

15 White handspun slub wool plied with machine spun yarn, and dyed fleece colours mixed and slub spun.

11 To ply handspun yarns together place each in a separate container and spin anti-clockwise.

16 Handspun wool plied with silk. The same hank before and after washing (left and right).

so they twist evenly together (11).

Wind the plied yarn into a hank for washing (12). Wash wool by squeezing it gently in warm soapy water, rinsing thoroughly and spin drying. You will be surprised by the difference (16).

Interesting threads can be made by allowing irregular quantities of fibre to pass into the thread when pulling out the yarn fibres for spinning. Slub yarns are made of thick and thin spinning at intervals along the length of the yarn (14). This is most effective when plied with a fine machine spun yarn and when there is more twist in the ply of the thin than the thick parts of the thread (15).

Wool fibres can be teased out, washed in warm soapy water, dyed and teased out again into a layer while still damp. By mixing the colours of the fibres when spinning, very exciting results can be obtained (15).

Using Chemical Dyes

1 Acetic acid for dyeing wool, silk and nylon. Common salt, wooden dowel, teaspoons and dye.

2 Test dyeing a sample of wool. Acetic acid and salt have been added to the dye liquor.

3 Test samples of mercerised and plain cotton, left and right, dyed together with direct dyes.

You will need:
Dye bath (enamel bowl, metal bucket or clothes boiler)
Small saucepan (samples, mixing)
Teaspoons for measuring
Smooth sticks (length of wooden dowel for stirring)
Dyestuff; Acetic acid (wool, silk)
Glaubers or common salt

Successful dyeing of yarn or fabric is regulated by the relationships between several factors: the nature of the fibre and the dye, the concentration and temperature of the dye bath, and the presence of salt and acetic acid to

encourage absorption of dye.

Chemical dyes do not react the same way with every fibre, for fibres vary in their readiness to absorb dyes, and some colours take more easily than others. Smoother lustrous fibres such as worsted, mohair, silk, mercerised cotton and viscose rayon will dye most easily, giving clear bright colours.

To determine the type of an unknown fibre in order to choose a suitable dyestuff, try some burning tests of the yarn. Wool, silk and worsted burn slowly with a strong smell like burning hair, and

leave a soft ash attached to the yarn. Cotton, mercerised cotton, linen, ramie, viscose rayon and other cellulose fibres burn quickly leaving a fine ash which falls away from the yarn. There is a smell like burning paper. Acetate rayon and all the chemical fibres withdraw from the flame and melt.

Pale shades may be difficult to dye evenly. Use the minimum of acid and salt. If dye levelling is uneven, try bringing the yarn back to simmer in clean water, then adding salt. If a colour becomes too dark, simmer in clean water and salt with more of

4 Hank of bouclé wool tied in a figure of eight at intervals prepared for dyeing for the blanket.

5 Suspend the hank above the dye bath with a different part of the hank immersed in the dye liquor.

6 Remove the hanks from the dye bath, thoroughly rinse and spin dry.

the same undyed fibres to absorb surplus dye. All fibres have a limit of dye absorption, and you cannot change a dark colour which has been fully dyed by adding more dye. Some pale shades of commercial yarn can change colour through over-dyeing.

Use a dye bath which is large enough for the yarn to be turned easily. For large quantities of yarn use two dye baths at once, constantly changing the hanks of yarn between the two baths. It is a good idea to start by using less dyestuff than you think you will need and adding more to get the right colour. Always remove yarn before adding more dyestuff or salt, and stir well.

Before dyeing a quantity of yarn for a project, you should dye small wrappings of yarn for samples (2, 3). Keep a note of the dye colour or mixture of colours used in each test.

Make your yarn into a hank by winding it round a hank winder, the end of a small table or legs of an upturned chair or stool. Tie the hanks with strong yarn using the same type of fibre if possible. Knot the loose ends together with an extra length of yarn round the hank. All ties should be loose

enough to allow dye to penetrate the yarn (4). After dyeing, dry and straighten hank, cut ties and wind yarn into a ball. A level teaspoon of dyestuff will dye a medium to dark shade on about 100 g (4 oz) yarn (dry weight). Always wet all yarn thoroughly before dyeing. Wash oiled wool in soap flakes to remove oil. Wool will matt and shrink in sudden changes of temperature or high concentrations of soap, so use plenty of water with soap, and never take yarn directly from a hot dye bath into cold water.

Acetic acid dyes
Clear, brilliant colours, excellent for pale shades, used for dyeing wool, worsted, silk, nylon.

Paste dyestuff with cold water, add boiling water and stir. Add two teaspoons acetic acid diluted with double the quantity of water. Add half the dissolved dyestuff to warm dye bath and stir. Add wet yarn to the dye bath, slowly raise the temperature, and simmer for 30-60 minutes. Stir gently to keep the yarn moving continuously. Add two teaspoons of salt at intervals to help fibres absorb dye. Add further dyestuff as required. When you have your

chosen colour, remove yarn, rinse thoroughly in warm water and spin dry. When dyeing silk do not allow the temperature to exceed 90°C as this will damage silk fibres. Use less acetic acid and no salt for nylon.

Direct dyes
Used for cotton, linen, rayon, mercerised cotton and other cellulose fibres, also painting or dyeing paper. Selected colours in direct dyes will also dye wool and silk and are sold for household use. Weigh and then wet yarn. Mix dyestuff into a paste with cold water, add boiling water and stir. Add dyestuff to a warm dye bath and stir. Add yarn to dye bath and slowly raise the temperature to boiling point keeping the yarn moving. Add two teaspoons of salt at intervals, and further dyestuff as required. Squeeze the dye liquor from a few threads to check colour. Unlike wool these fibres dry to a lighter shade. Simmer for 30-60 minutes, cool, rinse and spin dry.

Reactive dyes
Procion dyestuffs include CIBA and Reactone (Geigy). Used for dyeing cellulose fibres and also

7 Before dyeing it is advisable to do test samples for choice of colour and to see the effect.

8 Bind the two sections of warp for tie-dyeing together at intervals along the remainder of the warp.

9 Remove the warp from the dye bath, rinse, spin dry, and remove the raffia bindings.

wool and silk.

Hot dyeing Procion H brands: paste dyestuff with cold water. Dissolve in hot water and add to warm dye bath. Add yarn. Dye for 15 minutes and add salt. Dye for 15 minutes and add 20% washing soda. Dye for 30-60 minutes. Rinse in cold running water, wash in hot water and spin dry.

Cold dyeing Procion M brands: dissolve 25 g urea in 300 cc boiling water. Allow to cool and stir into dye. Add cold water. This solution will last three days. Before dyeing add 4 g washing soda, 8 g bicarbonate of soda and 88 cc cold water. Add yarn. This solution will last two hours. Rinse in cold running water, wash in hot water and spin dry.

Basic dyes
Used for wool and cellulose fibre. They give brilliant colour but are not colour fast. Straw, wood, raffia and paper may be dyed but will fade if exposed to direct sunlight. Mordant cotton, linen and viscose rayon before dyeing. Prepare mordant by dissolving 50 g (2 oz) tannic acid in 3 l (5 pt) of cold water. Soak the yarn for 24 hours or heat in the mordant bath to 60°C, leave to cool for two hours, squeeze and dry. Do not rinse the yarn. An excellent way to apply these dyes is to use them to give brilliance to a yarn previously dyed with direct dyes, which act as a mordant. For wool and silk, no mordant is required and the dyeing process is the same as acid dyes for silk.

Dispersal dyes
Polyester dyes used for acetate rayon, polyester and acrylic fibres. The dyestuff is not water soluble, but will form a fine suspension when stirred into warm water. The dye bath should contain hot water at 70°C, acetic acid, one teaspoonful of dispersant and two teaspoonfuls of accelerant per ½ l (1 pt) of liquid. Add prepared dyestuff and stir. Add yarn and boil for 30-60 minutes.

Dip-dyeing and tie-dyeing
These are simple dyeing processes giving a variety of colours or shades in sections of the hank of yarn. Prepare the dye bath and bring to the boil with salt added. Thoroughly wet the yarn.

For dip-dyeing: suspend the hank of yarn above the dye bath with part immersed in the dye liquor and simmer for 7-30 minutes (5). Prepare another dye bath at the boil with a different colour dyestuff and salt added, and immerse a different part of your hank in this (5). Repeat the process until the required effect is achieved. Remove the yarn, rinse thoroughly and spin dry.

Always dye the light shades first. An inevitable running of the dyes produces a gradation of new shades between colours. Use this method to dye the sisal string for your rya door mat (page 29-31). Using direct yellow and turquoise dye will produce green between these colours (6).

Tie-dyeing is more time consuming than dip-dyeing, but sharp changes of colour can be achieved and small areas of yarn can be controlled in dyeing. Bind the hanks of yarn tightly with raffia at intervals (8). Bind further sections and add more dyestuff to create a range of tones or a mixture of colours. Use this method to dye the yarn for your purple cushion covers (page 38-39).

List of Suppliers

Great Britain

Craftsman's Mark Ltd.
Trefnant
Denbigh, North Wales

Dryad Ltd.
Northgates
Leicester (mail order)
178 Kensington High Street
London W8 (retail)

Harris Looms
Dept Z.
Northgrove Road
Hawkhurst, Kent

Frank Herring & Sons
27 High Street West
Dorchester, Dorset

Eliza Leadbeater
Rookery Cottage
Dalefords Lane
Whitegate
Northwich, Cheshire

Lillstina Looms
Granville House
6 Granville Street
Winsford, Cheshire

Uni-dye
P.O. Box No 10
Ilkley, Yorkshire

U.S.A.

Berga/Ullman Inc.
P.O. Box 831
Ossining
N.Y. 10562

Colonial Woolen Mills Inc.
6501 Barberton Avenue
Cleveland
Ohio 44102

Earth Guild Inc.
15 Tudor Street
Cambridge
Mass. 02139

Frederick J Fawcett Inc.
129 South Street
Boston
Mass. 02111

Lillstina Looms
P.O. Box 1373
Binghampton
N.Y. 13902

School Products Co., Inc.
312 East 23rd Street
New York
N.Y. 10010

The Spinning Wheel
130 Church Street
San Francisco
Calif. 94114

Thought Products Inc.
R.D.2, Route 219
North Somerset,
Pa. 15501

Some further reading

A Handbook of Weaves
G. H. Oelsner,
Dover Publications, N.Y. 1974;
Constable, London.

A Handweaver's Pattern Book
Marguerite Porter Davison,
Marguerite P. Davison
Publishers,
U.S.A.

Band Weaving
Harold and Sylvia Tacker,
Studio Vista, London, 1974.

Foundations of Weaving
Mike Halsey and
Lore Youngmark,
David and Charles,
Newton Abbot,
Devon, 1975.

From Fibres to Fabrics
Elizabeth Gale, Mills and Boon,
London, 1971.

Handspinning
Allen Fannin, Van Nostrand
Reinhold, New York, 1970.

Handspinning
Eliza Leadbeater, Studio Vista,
London, 1976;
Branford, New York.

Inkle Loom Weaving
Nina Holland, Pitman, London,
1973.

Off the Loom
Shirley Marein, Studio Vista,
London, 1972.

On Weaving
Anni Albers, Studio Vista,
London, 1974.

Simple Weaving
Hilary Chetwynd, Studio Vista,
London, 1969.

Tapestry as an Art Form
Theo Moorman, Van Nostrand
Reinhold, New York, 1975.

*Weaving – a Handbook for Fiber
Craftsmen* Shirley E. Held, Holt,
Rinehart & Winston Inc.,
New York, 1973.

Publications

Crafts
Crafts Advisory Committee
28 Haymarket
London SW1

Craft Horizons
American Crafts Council
44 West 53rd Street
New York, N.Y. 10019

Shuttle, Spindle and Dyepot
Handweavers Guild of America Inc.
998 Farmington Avenue
West Hartford
Conn. 06107

*Weavers Journal, Association
of Guilds of Weavers,
Spinners and Dyers*
c/o Federation of
British Crafts Society,
80a Southampton Row,
London WC1B 4BA.

Acknowledgements

Dyes by courtesy of Uni-dye
Four Shaft Loom by courtesy of
Harris Looms